MILLIE STAMM

BESIDE STILL WATERS

MEDITATION MOMENTS
ON THE PSALMS

Zondervan Publishing House
Grand Rapids, Michigan

Daybreak Books are published by the Zondervan Publishing House
1415 Lake Drive, S.E., Grand Rapids, Michigan 49506

BESIDE STILL WATERS

Stamm, Millie.
Beside still waters.

  1. Bible. O.T. Psalms—Meditations. I. Title.
BS1430.4.S72 1983   242'.5   83-19768
ISBN 0-310-33062-9

Unless otherwise indicated, all Scripture is from the King James Version.

Compiled by Julie Ackerman Link
Designed by Ann Cherryman

Printed in the United States of America

    91 92 93 94 95 / EE / 10 9

Foreword

The universal experiences of humanity—suffering, sorrow, sin, celebration—are best expressed through poetry. And the poetry of David and the other psalmists, who revealed themselves to God with such honesty and poignancy that subsequent generations have been able to see themselves in each marvelous stanza, is as eloquent as any that can be found.

Not all of us are poets or musicians, as was David. But all of us have experienced times of despair and longing, as well as times of great joy and triumph. David says for all of us what we cannot find the words to say.

These meditations on the Psalms come from Millie Stamm's two popular devotional books, *Meditation Moments* and *Be Still and Know*. We offer them for comfort, for instruction, and for the confirmation of what David knew so well: our God controls every circumstance.

THE PUBLISHER

Psalm 1:2

But his delight is in the law of the Lord; and in his law doth he meditate day and night.

Meditation is defined as "contemplation; reflection; contemplation on sacred matters as a devotional act."

The English word for meditation comes from the Latin word, "meditor," meaning to think over, consider, contemplate, reflect upon.

The source of our meditation is the Word of God. David said, "O how love I thy law! it is my meditation all the day" (Ps. 119:97).

Meditation is more than just Bible reading. It begins with the reading of it but continues in contemplating or considering the truth as revealed in it. "Thy testimonies are my meditation" (Ps. 119:99). "I will meditate in thy precepts, and have respect unto thy ways" (Ps. 119:15). "Thy servant did meditate in thy statutes" (Ps. 119:23).

The Bible gives a direct command to meditate. Paul said to Timothy, "Meditate upon these things. . . ." (1 Tim. 4:15).

Meditation on God's Word gives spiritual illumination. "The entrance of thy words giveth light" (Ps. 119:130). Meditation on God's Word allows the Heavenly light to break in upon our inner darkness. Only the light of the Word is strong enough to dispel spiritual darkness.

We need to gain knowledge from God's Word, but through meditation on it, it becomes a part of our life.

Meditation is essential for the person God can really

use. When Joshua was to replace Moses as leader of the children of Israel, God said to him, "This book of the law shall not depart out of thy mouth; but thou shalt meditate therein day and night, that thou mayest observe to do according to all that is written therein" (Josh. 1:8).

George Mueller, the great man of God, said that at first he began his devotional time with prayer. Then he would read and meditate on God's Word. Later he discovered that his spiritual life deepened when he reversed the order. He opened his Bible first, asking God to give him illumination on it. Then he would read and meditate on it. And finally he would have his prayer time. This led him to a greater life in the power of God.

In meditation we bring ". . . into captivity every thought to the obedience of Christ" (2 Cor. 10:5).

Psalm 1:3

And he shall be like a tree planted by the rivers of water, that bringeth forth his fruit in his season; his leaf also shall not wither; and whatsoever he doeth shall prosper.

We are familiar with the poem that ends with the line, "But only God can make a tree." The psalmist compares the Christian to a tree, a God-made tree.

We are *planted* trees—"he shall be like a tree planted." When we plant a tree we select the spot where we want it and the type of tree best suited for that location and for the purpose we have in mind. God knows where He wants to plant us and He has a purpose in planting us there. It may not be the place of our choice but it is the place of His choosing.

God *provides* for His trees—He plants them "by the rivers of water." Wherever we are planted, God's River of Life flows by. Our roots can reach down and constantly draw nourishment from it. We must drink of it regularly.

We are to be *productive* trees—". . . that bringeth forth his fruit in his season." We must be productive in due season, bringing forth God's fruit in God's season. "When our lives take deep rootage in Christ, we will bring forth rich fruitage for Him."

God's trees will be *perpetually alive*—"his leaf also shall not wither." We will be ever living, trees of unfading beauty radiating the loveliness of our lovely Lord. God's Word says of Him, "He is altogether lovely." One definition for "altogether" is "permanently." So in Him we are permanently lovely.

We are *prosperous* trees—"whatsoever he doeth shall prosper." We mature in Him. Rooted in Christ, nourished by the Word and refreshed by the Spirit, our lives become blessings to others.

Psalm 1:6

For the Lord knoweth the way of righteousness.

How often we have heard this: "I do not know what tomorrow holds but I know who holds tomorrow." He knows our way through this day, this month, this year. The word "way" in this verse means "trodden path." But Joshua 3:4 reads, "For ye have not passed this way heretofore." If we have not taken this way before, how can it be a trodden path for us?

One night we had a snowstorm. The next morning I watched our neighbor with her two small girls and two neighbor boys playing "Follow the Leader" in the snow. She went ahead of them as their leader, making a trodden path in the snow. As long as they followed in her path they had no trouble. But when they left the path, they stumbled and fell.

In our Christian lives we can follow our Leader, who is the Lord, "simply fixing our gaze upon Jesus, our *Prince Leader* in the faith" (Weymouth). The way ahead is unknown to us, for we have not taken it before. But as we follow our Leader who goes before us, it becomes a trodden path for us.

Today does your way ahead look dark? Are the clouds hanging low? Are there shadows surrounding you? Your Leader, Jesus Christ, knows your way ahead. Keep your eyes on Him and your unknown way will become a trodden path as you follow Him.

Psalm 2:8

Ask of me, and I shall give thee the heathen for thine inheritance.

In this Psalm, God the Father, the Son and the Holy Spirit are speaking together. In verse 8 the Father speaks to the Son, saying, "Ask of me, and I shall give thee the heathen [or the unbelieving] for thine inheritance."

Today we have a share in the work the Father gave to the Son. We read in 2 Peter 3:9, "The Lord . . . is not willing that any should perish, but that all should come to repentance." We, too, are to come to Him in prayer, asking Him for the unbelieving. We are to ask Him to bring others into a personal relationship with Jesus Christ. This is conditional—"Ask of me [our part], and I shall give thee [God's part]." Are you asking today? How many do you have on your prayer list?

Perhaps you need to ask God to give you a renewed and enlarged vision of those about you who need spiritual help—of the many around the world who do not know Jesus Christ. "Where there is no vision, the people perish" (Prov. 29:18).

A few years ago several missionaries in Korea decided to meet together at noon each day for prayer, asking God to bless their work. At the end of a month they saw no results, so one of them suggested that they discontinue their prayer meeting and pray at home. Does this sound familiar? However, the others were convinced that they should continue to pray even more faithfully, which they did for several months. Finally, the Spirit of God moved in their midst, and many lives were transformed. One of the missionaries said, "It paid well to spend several months in prayer, for when God began to work, more was accomplished in half a day than all of the missionaries could have accomplished in half a year."

As we pray, asking for the unbelieving, God will work in hearts, drawing them to Himself.

Psalm 3:3

But thou, O Lord, art a shield for me; my glory, and the lifter up of my head.

King David was facing a time of great distress. His son, Absalom, had led a successful revolt against him.

David, in deep despair, prayed, "Lord, how are they increased that trouble me! many are they that rise up against me. Many there be which say of my soul, 'There is no help for him in God.' Selah" (Ps. 3:1,2). His cause seemed hopeless.

But David knew where to go in time of trouble. He turned in confidence to God, his PRESENT source of help. "But THOU, O LORD, art [right now] a shield to me; my glory, and the lifter up of my head."

When the darts of his enemies were hurled at him, God was his shield. In the midst of his discouragement, he knew the glory of God's presence. God's presence was so real to him he could say of Him, "My glory." Even though he was downcast, God lifted his head, delivering him from despair.

David took his burden to the Lord and left it with Him. Because of his confident trust in God, he could say, "I laid me down and slept; I awaked; for the LORD sustained me" (v. 5).

Does your case seem hopeless? Do you feel everyone has turned against you? You have the same source of help at such times as David. "But THOU, O LORD."

We need not fear the attacks of the enemy for God surrounds us and protects us with Himself as our mighty shield. His presence within becomes our glory, bringing His beauty and splendor into our lives. When our heads and hearts are bowed down, our eyes overflowing with tears, He lovingly and tenderly lifts up our heads so we can see HIM. As we look into His face, we are comforted by Him. He wipes away our tears.

When we commit our problems to Him, we can say as David did, "I cried unto the Lord with my voice, and he heard me out of his holy hill. Selah" (v. 4). Then we can lie down and sleep, for we know, "The LORD sustained me" (v. 5).

Psalm 3:4

I cried unto the Lord with my voice, and he heard me out of his holy hill. Selah.

Throughout the Psalms we find the word "Selah." One day I discovered a meaning that brought new appreciation and understanding of its use in Scripture.

"Selah" is a musical word, meaning in the Hebrew "rest," "pause," "a lifting up." In the temple music there would be a rest for the singers while the instruments continued playing. In the *Amplified Bible* "Selah" is translated "pause, and calmly think of that."

God put rests in David's life that he might "pause and calmly think" that—God helps, God hears, and God blesses. David said, "Many are saying of me, There is no help for him in God" (Ps. 3:2, *Amplified*). In the rest stops of his life David had learned by experience that "God has helped ME. Selah—pause and calmly think of that."

Not only did God help David, but He heard his cries in time of need. David could say, "God heard ME. Selah—pause and calmly think of that."

David recognized God's blessing on his life. "Your blessing be upon Your people" (v. 8, *Amplified*). He could say, "God has blessed ME. Selah—pause and calmly think of that."

What God did for David, He will do for us. At times we, too, need to experience a "Selah" in our lives, a time when we pause and rest. To be still and rest is good therapy for today's fast pace of living. The heart strings may be taut, even on the verge of snapping. Suddenly, God inserts a "Selah," a rest, that we might pause and calmly think of Him. As we lift our souls to Him, we are refreshed. The tension lessens, we gain a deeper view of God's goodness, and He becomes more real.

May we not miss the blessing God has for us in our "Selahs"—the times of rest and refreshing in our lives. Someone has said, "There is no music in a rest, but there is the making of music in it."

Today we can pause and calmly think—God helps ME, God hears ME, and God blesses ME.

Psalm 4:1

Hear me when I call, O God of my righteousness; thou hast enlarged me when I was in distress; have mercy upon me, and hear my prayer.

David lived within calling distance of God. In time of need he lifted his SUPPLICATIONS to God. He recognized that out of his distress good could come. "You have freed me when I was hemmed in and enlarged me when I was in distress; have mercy upon me and hear my prayer" (*Amplified*). Someone has said, "God allowed David to be in distress for He wanted to make him a bigger man for bigger tasks."

God had SET APART David for His own. "But know that the Lord hath set apart him that is godly for himself" (Ps. 4:3). God has set us apart, too, for Himself, not because of who we are or what we are, but because of what we can become in Christ.

David could have become bitter, thinking of his foes. Instead, he said, "Stand in awe, and sin not; commune with your own heart upon your bed, and be STILL" (v. 4). As he became still within, he could hear God's gentle whisperings to him during the night watches.

David recognized the SECURITY of trusting the Lord. "Put your trust in the Lord" (v. 5). People may forsake you, circumstances may change. But God never forsakes. We can trust Him at all times.

In spite of his troubles, David experienced a SATIS-FIED HEART, one filled with God-given gladness. "Yes, the gladness you have given me is far greater than their joys at harvest time as they gaze at their bountiful crops" (Ps. 4:7, LB). Too often we look for joy and gladness in prosperity. But the gladness David wrote about had its source in God. It is a "more than" gladness in the midst of trials, a gladness dependent on God.

Trusting God, he could say, "I will lie down in peace and sleep, for though I am alone, O Lord, you will keep me safe" (v. 8, LB).

Regardless of our problems today, our hearts can be filled with a God-given gladness that completely satisfies.

Psalm 4:7

Thou hast put gladness in my heart, more than in the time that their corn and their wine increased.

David had been going through deep waters. At a time when friends and family had deserted him, he could have become despondent. But, no! He writes of the gladness he had in his heart.

Too often we assume that joy and gladness come from prosperity. It is not difficult to be glad when everything is going our way and we have all we need. But this is not the gladness about which David was writing. The source of this joy was in God—"*Thou* hast put gladness in my heart." It is a gladness that results from an inner peace of heart.

The "corn and wine" increase of material things does not put this kind of gladness in our hearts. David didn't mean that he had no material blessings. He didn't mean that one cannot have gladness of heart if he has possessions. But he did mean that the Lord was far more precious and wonderful to him than anything he owned. God gave him a "more than" gladness in the midst of troubles and trials. This gladness was entirely independent of circumstances.

Do we have this kind of gladness—a gladness that does not depend on what we have or what we do?—a gladness that does not depend on friends, on where we live, on praise or on circumstances? This gladness comes from God Himself and it is for His own dear children.

Psalm 5:3

My voice shalt thou hear in the morning, O Lord; in the morning will I direct my prayer unto thee, and will look up.

What a privilege to begin the day in the presence of God! It has been said, "The morning is one end of the thread on which the day's activities are strung and should be well-knotted with devotion." It makes a difference when we look into the face of God before going out to face people.

Here we read something about David's prayer life. Out of a heart of love and worship he directed his prayer to God at the beginning of the day. He *lifted* his *voice* to God in prayer. "Hearken unto the voice of my cry. . . . My voice shalt thou hear in the morning" (vv. 2, 3a). He began his day talking to God, confident that He would hear and answer.

Not only did the psalmist lift his voice, but he *lifted his heart* also. "In the morning will I direct my prayer unto thee." In the original Hebrew the expression "direct my prayer" implies coming to God with a prepared heart, a heart quieted from the hustle and bustle of the day, ready to listen to Him. Often we rush into and out of His presence without that quiet preparation of heart which is essential to communion with Him. "In the morning I prepare [a prayer, a sacrifice] for You, and watch and wait [for You to speak to my heart]" (v. 3, *Amplified*). *Lift* your *heart* with your *voice* to God.

David's eyes followed the direction of his voice and heart: "and will *look up*." We may lift our voices to God but keep our eyes focused on our problems, our needs, our weaknesses and disappointments. When we *lift* our *eyes,* we see Him. "And when they had lifted up their eyes, they saw no man, save *Jesus only*" (Matt. 17:8).

Psalm 8:3, 4

When I consider thy heavens, the work of thy fingers, the moon and the stars, which thou hast ordained; what is man, that thou art mindful of him? and the son of man, that thou visitest him?

One evening my husband and I were sitting in our back yard. As the stars came out we tried to count them as we had done in our childhood. Of course we soon lost count, but I remembered that God's Word says, "He telleth the number of the stars; he calleth them all by their names" (Ps. 147:4).

Can you not visualize David as he sat on the hillside and looked at the starry heavens, meditating on the glory of it all? Contemplating man and his place in this great universe, he questions, "What is man, that thou art mindful of him? and the son of man, that thou visitest him?"

God is *"mindful"* of us. This two-syllable word consists of the words *"mind"* and *"full."* Have you not looked down on the earth from an airplane or a high building and realized that man is only a speck in God's great universe? Yet the psalmist says that God's mind is *full* of man. The God of the universe is also the God of the individual. His thoughts are centered in man and his needs. He is more interested in us than in the rest of His creation.

God proved how interested He is in us—He visited us in the *person of His Son*. "And the Word was made flesh, and dwelt among us" (John 1:14a). "For God so loved the world, that he gave his only begotten Son, that whosoever believeth in him should not perish, but have everlasting life" (John 3:16).

Psalm 16:5

The Lord is the portion of mine inheritance. . . .

This is a day of materialism—a day when "things" seem to be very important in our lives. While the world scrambles madly for material gain, the believer can say with the psalmist, "The Lord is the portion of mine inheritance."

David is here speaking of the portion which belonged to the priesthood tribe of Levi. When the land of Canaan was distributed among the tribes of Israel, the tribe of Levi received no part of it. We read in Joshua 13:33, "But unto the tribe of Levi Moses gave not any inheritance: the Lord God of Israel was their inheritance, as he said unto them." They were to serve the Lord and be sustained by the supply of the Temple. The Lord Himself was their portion and would care for them. The word "portion" is defined as "allotment" or "share from an estate."

The portion of our inheritance—the Lord Jesus Christ—is available today for everyone who has a personal relationship with Him. Our portion of this inheritance includes His life, His strength, His peace, His joy—all that He is, is available to us. Thus each of us can say, "Thou art *my* portion, O Lord: I have said that I would keep thy words" (Ps. 119:57). It is an everlasting portion: "God is the strength of my heart, and *my portion for ever*" (Ps. 73:26b).

Someone has said, "Faith in Christ is the key that unlocks the cabinet of His promises and empties out their treasures into the soul."

Psalm 18:1

I will love thee, O Lord, my strength.

These verses reveal the intimate relationship of the psalmist David to his God. How God's heart must have rejoiced to hear David say, "I will love thee." God delights to have us come humbly into His presence, taking time to love Him. When was the last time you paused and told Him, "O Lord, I do love you"?

When we love someone dearly, and we know they love us, we have complete trust in them. David said, "The Lord . . . in whom I will trust" (v. 2). Then he enumerated several things God is to the person that trusts Him:

"The Lord is my rock"; a rock is a foundation. "The Lord is my fortress"; a fortress is a place of shelter and safety. "The Lord is my deliverer"; how often we try every human source of deliverance before turning to the Lord. "The Lord is my strength"; not He gives strength—He *is* Strength—*my* strength. "The Lord is my buckler"; a shield to protect one from the enemy. "The Lord is the horn of my salvation"; in the Hebrew the word for *horn* and *shone* are the same. When David spoke of the Lord as the horn of his salvation, he recognized that the Lord was the light and glory of his life. "The Lord is my high tower"; there is safety for us in the tower. God was very personal to David; each time he said *"my."*

First, he expressed his love to the Lord, then his trust in the One he loves. Because he trusts Him, he has confidence in calling on Him for help. "I will call upon the Lord, who is worthy to be praised; so shall I be saved from mine enemies."

He *is* worthy to be praised.

Psalm 18:30

As for God, his way is perfect.

Today our hearts can be encouraged as we recognize the truth of this verse. We may wonder about certain things that have happened to us. Our path may be dark ahead and we cannot see our way. It may be blocked by obstacles that we cannot see around. A sorrow may have clouded our sky. The plan of our life may have been completely changed. We may not know which way to turn. We may be wondering what is best for us.

When we commit our way to Him, it becomes His way. Then we can be sure that whether it is joy or sorrow, sunshine or clouds, health or sickness, plenty or want, His way for us IS perfect. We cannot doubt that. He sees the end from the beginning. He sees the pattern He is working out in our lives and will not make one mistake. We may not understand it, but He does. That is enough. Can we say, not with a sigh, but with a song— "perfect is His way" (Ps. 18:30, *Berkeley*).

Not only is God's way perfect, but He makes our way perfect. "It is God that . . . MAKETH MY way perfect" (v. 32). Perfect means "fulfill" or "complete." He completes or fulfills our life and brings it into conformity with His will. There is a making process necessary to perfect His way in us. It is the making process against which we often rebel.

A woman was complaining about the hardness of her life with all its trials and troubles. She said to someone, "I wish I had never been made." "My dear," replied her friend, "you are not yet made. You are only being made and you are quarreling with God's process."

He enables us to surmount our difficulties. As we yield ourselves to Him, He will complete the process of making our way perfect.

"For my thoughts are not your thoughts, neither are your ways my ways, saith the Lord. For as the heavens are higher than the earth, so are my ways higher than your ways, and my thoughts than your thoughts" (Isa. 55:8, 9).

Psalm 19:7

God's laws are perfect. They protect us, make us wise, and give us joy and light. (LB)

As we see the beauty of the world about us, our thoughts turn to the God who created it in all its glory and majesty. In the first six verses of Psalm 19 the greatness of God is revealed in the WORK of His creation. "The heavens declare the glory of God, and the firmament shows and proclaims His handiwork" (Ps. 19:1, *Amplified*). The heavens do not point to themselves, but to the work of another.

In verses 7 through 11, God is revealed in His WORD. Only in the Scriptures do we learn of His redemptive plan for mankind. In it is revealed the resources of God designed for the inner life of man.

As the psalmist considered God's Word, he enumerated some of the attributes of God's Word and some of its effects in our lives.

It is perfect—without flaw or defect. It is complete. It

accomplishes everything it needs to. It convicts of sin, pointing to the Savior. It restores the soul, refreshing the inner life. "It restores the whole person" (Ps. 19:7, LB).

It is the sure Word of God, reliable, trustworthy to follow, giving us wisdom and direction.

His Word is right. It leads us in a straight path to our goal in Christ. It rejoices the heart, delighting those who obey it, bringing the joy of the Lord into each heart.

It is the pure Word, purifying us as we allow it to be personally applied to our lives. It enlightens, illuminating the dark for us, clarifying our vision as we walk in obedience to it.

It is clean, a cleansing agent for our lives. It has an enduring quality, preventing us from defiling ourselves.

It is true and righteous, ever faithful. It reveals His holiness and justice. It shows that He is right in all He does.

The Word of God has its proper place in our lives when we allow it to accomplish for us and in us what God intended it to. Are we giving it proper place in our lives?

Psalm 19:10

More to be desired are they than gold, yea, than much fine gold; sweeter also than the honey and the honeycomb.

It has been said, "We must know the Word of God to know the God of the Word." The universe reveals the handiwork of God, but the Bible reveals the heart of God. The Word has a great effect on our lives, enriching them as we read and meditate on it.

A great value is put on the teaching of the Bible. David

said, "More to be desired are they than gold, yea, than much fine gold." If you were to list your valuable possessions, would you include your Bible? Its POSSESSION is better than gold.

His Word brings abiding PLEASURE to those who search its pages. ". . . sweeter also than honey and the honeycomb." Have you had a special need and when you opened the Bible and read from it, it was sweet to your taste as it met your need? It is a PROTECTION, warning us of temptations and pitfalls, and rewarding those who obey it. "Moreover by them is thy servant warned" (Ps. 19:11). There is PROFIT in keeping it. ". . . in keeping of them there is great reward."

Do you want to know more of God? Then turn to His Word. Let Him reveal Himself from its pages. The Holy Spirit will make the one revealed in His Word real in your life.

When Alexander Duff sailed for India as a missionary, he took a library of eight hundred books, much treasured by him. In a shipwreck he lost all of them. Looking back to the sea, he saw something small being washed ashore. Picking it up, he discovered it was his own Bible. He decided God was showing him that the Bible was worth more than all the other volumes of his library. Through his study of the Word, God became more real to him, and his life was a great blessing to the people of India.

The Bible is the only Book whose Author is always present when one reads it.

Psalm 19:14

Let the words of my mouth, and the meditation of my heart, be acceptable in thy sight, O Lord, my strength, and my redeemer.

In Psalm 19 David wrote of God's great and glorious power revealed in the heavens and the earth. What beauty we see displayed in His Creation! What power is demonstrated! David also wrote of the divinely revealed and inspired Word of God.

Then David closed the Psalm with a very familiar prayer. As he lifted his voice in worship to God, he asked God to control both his inner and outer life.

First, David prayed that the words of his mouth would be acceptable to God. Suppose we made a tape of all the words we speak each day and at night before retiring we would play the tape back. Would we be pleased with what we heard? Or would we be surprised to hear the words we had spoken during the day? Would they be gentle, kind, loving, comforting, encouraging? Or would they be harsh, bitter, unkind, critical?

But David continued to pray that not only his words but even the meditations of his heart be acceptable to God. He knew his words indicated the condition of his heart; that the outer expressions of a life in words and actions come from an inner attitude of heart and mind. Matthew 12:34 says, ". . . out of the abundance of the heart the mouth speaketh." The *Living Bible* reads, "For a man's heart determines his speech." If our heart is right with God, our words will be acceptable to God, and our conversation will please Him. David was more desirous of pleasing God than people.

He cried out to God, "Search me, O God, and know my heart: try me, and know my thoughts: and see if there be any wicked way in me, and lead me in the way everlasting" (Ps. 139:23, 24).

What about our conversation today? Is it acceptable to God? Are our thoughts pleasing to Him? What are the meditations of our hearts?

May our prayer be that the words of our mouth—what we say; and the meditations of our hearts—what we do; reveal an inner and outer life that is acceptable and pleasing to God.

Psalm 23:1

The Lord is my shepherd; I shall not want.

Little words often have great significance. In the above verse the personal pronoun "MY" is important. The little two-letter word indicates a relationship between the Lord and David. David didn't say the Lord is "a" shepherd, but "my" shepherd.

Sheep easily go astray. It takes the shepherd's careful search to find them and restore them to the fold. "All we like sheep have gone astray; we have turned every one to his own way; and the Lord hath laid on him the iniquity of us all" (Isa. 53:6).

Jesus Christ came as the Good Shepherd to make possible a personal relationship between God and man. Jesus said, "I am the good shepherd; the good shepherd giveth his life for the sheep" (John 10:11).

One of England's leading actors was being honored at a banquet. After dinner the Master of Ceremonies asked the actor if he would recite for the guests. He consented, asking if there was something in particular someone would like to hear. After a moment's pause, an old clergyman spoke up, saying, "Sir, could you recite the Twenty-third Psalm?"

For a moment the actor was speechless. Then he said, "Yes, I will be glad to, but on one condition; that is, that after I have recited it, you will do the same."

Impressively the great actor recited the Psalm, holding his audience spellbound. As he finished, a great burst of applause broke forth from the guests.

After the applause ceased, the clergyman quietly arose. The audience listened as the Psalm was given. When it was done, there was not a dry eye in the room.

After a moment of silence, the actor said, "I reached your ears, but this man reached your hearts. I know the Psalm, but he knows the Shepherd."

Do you only know the Psalm, or do you know the Shepherd? Can you say, "The Lord is MY Shepherd"? If not, would you like to invite Jesus Christ into your life to become your personal Savior and Good Shepherd?

"But as many as received him, to them gave he power to become the sons of God, even to them that believe on his name" (John 1:12).

Psalm 23:2

He maketh me to lie down in green pastures: he leadeth me beside the still waters.

The shepherd is at the very center of the life of the sheep. He provides for their every need, satisfying them completely.

Sheep will not lie down if they have cause to be fearful. They are easily frightened. However, as soon as the shepherd appears and moves in the midst of the restless flock, they become quiet.

The lives of many Christians are filled with fear, bringing restlessness and frustration. Our Good Shepherd appears, saying, "Fear THOU not; for I am with thee" (Isa. 41:10). His presence in the midst of our need removes fear and gives rest.

Sheep will not lie down if they are hungry. The shepherd searches for the best pasture land available for his sheep. Our Good Shepherd knows we need to be well nourished for inner satisfaction. He provides nourishment for us from the green pastures of His Word. Nourished by it, we can lie down in quiet contentment.

Occasionally He has to MAKE us lie down. It may take illness, loneliness, heartache, or sorrow to accomplish this.

Not only does the shepherd lead his sheep in the green meadows of nourishment and rest, but beside the still waters. We are refreshed at the waters of quietness. The word for "still" waters can be translated "stilled" waters. Sheep will not drink from a rushing stream. They instinctively know that if their coat of wool becomes wet, they could drown. Sometimes the shepherd builds a little dam in a rushing stream to enable the flock to drink from "stilled" waters.

At times the swift moving streams of life almost engulf us. God has to dam up a quiet stream where we can come and drink deeply of the Water of Life. We may discover that the very circumstances dreaded most bring spiritual refreshment.

Our Good Shepherd loves to see His sheep contented and relaxed, refreshed and satisfied with Him.

Today are you nourished and refreshed? Are you fully satisfied? "Blessed are they which do hunger and thirst after righteousness: for they shall be filled" (Matt. 5:6).

Psalm 23:3

He restoreth my soul: he leadeth me in the paths of righteousness for his name's sake.

Sheep stray easily. It is the shepherd's business to find the ones who have strayed and restore them to the fold.

Like sheep, we, too, go astray. At first we take one step away from the Good Shepherd, then another one. Before we realize what has happened, we have strayed from God's path of righteousness to a way of our own making.

Then we need the restoring touch of our Good Shepherd. The Hebrew word for restore means, "to turn about." We need to turn from our way to His.

David wrote from his own experience. He remembered a time when he had strayed and was out of fellowship with the Lord. He cried to God, "Restore unto me the joy of thy salvation" (Ps. 51:12). In His faithfulness, the Good Shepherd brought him back into fellowship with God.

In Isaiah 42:3 we read, "A bruised reed shall he not break." Shepherds in olden days played on reeds. They were easily broken and could not be mended. It was easy to make another, so the shepherd would snap it in two, throw it away, and make a new one. Our Shepherd does not do this. When the music is gone out of our soul, God does not snap us in two and throw us away—He mends and restores.

To guard against straying from His care, we need to spend time with Him, keeping close to His heart of love.

Some shepherds take time to be alone with each of their sheep every day. While grazing, one by one the sheep leave their pasture and go to the shepherd. He pats the sheep, rubs it, and lets it know it is very special to him.

If sheep have need of time alone with their shepherd daily, how much more important it is for us to spend time with our Shepherd. Keeping close TO Him keeps us from straying FROM Him. We are special to Him and He loves to have this close, intimate time with each of His children.

"I have loved thee with an everlasting love" (Jer. 31:3).

Psalm 23:4

Yea, though I walk through the valley of the shadow of death, I will fear no evil; for thou art with me; thy rod and thy staff they comfort me.

Sometimes the shepherd leads his sheep through dark, deep valleys where dangers lurk, where robbers and wild animals hide. Yet the sheep need not fear, for their shepherd watches over them.

The above Scripture verse does not say, "the valley of death," but "the valley of the shadow of death." Does this not include our entire earthly pilgrimage which finally leads to our heavenly home? On our way we may go through such valleys as fear and darkness.

We can walk through these valleys with confidence when we have the COMPANIONSHIP of the Shepherd; "I will fear no evil, for THOU art with me."

In Palestine when a shepherd moves his sheep to a higher pasture, often he has to take them through a valley. Our valley experiences lead us to "higher ground" in our spiritual experience.

Not only do the sheep have the companionship of the Shepherd, but the COMFORT of his rod and his staff. They are the weapons he uses as he leads them through the valley. The rod is used on the enemies, the staff on the sheep.

"Your rod [to protect] and Your staff [to guide], they comfort me" (Ps. 23:4, *Amplified*).

The rod is the symbol of His defending power. It is the weapon He uses to strike down the adversaries in our way. We need to transfer the responsibility of our safety to Him and stay close behind Him.

The shepherd uses the staff to keep his sheep from wandering, to draw them back into the way when they do, to lift them from places of danger into which they have fallen, and for correction.

There are many lessons we learn as we travel through the valley. Through them we have a greater appreciation and love for the Good Shepherd.

How we can thank Him for the companionship of His Presence and the Comfort of His rod and staff as we travel with Him!

Psalm 23:5

Thou preparest a table before me in the presence of mine enemies.

The psalmist has such an awareness of dependence upon his Good Shepherd. Through his life experiences he had learned that there is no want to the one who trusts his life to the Good Shepherd and walks close to Him.

As our Host, the Good Shepherd invites us to His table which He has provided and placed before us. He has taken utmost care to prepare His very best, amply providing for our every need. "And my God will liberally supply (fill to the full) your every need according to His riches in glory in Christ Jesus" (Phil. 4:19, *Amplified*).

The pastures where the sheep grazed in the Holy Land often had poisonous plants and dangerous animals. The shepherds would go before the sheep, digging out the dangerous plants and driving away animals that might harm the sheep.

Then the Good Shepherd prepares a table for us, with Himself as our Host. Because His meals are well-balanced, we are always satisfied at His table. "And Jesus said unto them, I am the bread of life: he that cometh to me shall never hunger; and he that believeth on me shall never thirst" (John 6:35). What a wonderful thought that daily we are His special care and that daily He is serving us.

We may be surrounded by enemies of doubt, fear, envy, self-pity, and rebellion. But in the midst of them our loving Host has prepared our daily provisions.

At His table there is a never-ending supply. His provisions never fail. "There is no want to them that fear him . . . they that seek the Lord shall not want any good thing" (Ps. 34:9, 10).

God's banqueting table is set before us. It is a table for our spiritual nourishment and refreshment. The food is not prepared ahead of time so it becomes stale, but just when needed so it is fresh. All we need is provided for us in the person of His Son, Jesus Christ.

This table is placed before us for our benefit. If we are to be nourished by God and His Son, we must partake of them. Are you nourished by them?

Psalm 23:5

Thou anointest my head with oil; my cup runneth over.

In Eastern countries it was customary not only to bathe the feet of guests as they arrived, but to pour fragrant oil on their heads, as a gesture of love and welcome.

Throughout Scripture, oil is a symbol of the Holy Spirit. No service is fruitful unless done in the power of the Holy Spirit. The Holy Spirit not only reflects the presence of Christ from our lives, but emits the fragrance of Jesus Christ, the Rose of Sharon. Another work of the Holy Spirit is to counteract irritations in our lives.

At certain times of year, sheep are troubled by nose flies and parasites. The shepherd uses an ointment containing oil to rub on their noses and heads as a protection.

This is illustrated in our lives by the fact that we become annoyed by the irritations in our lives. The Spirit of God can counteract these aggravations of personality conflicts and other frustrations that torment us. He has the power to overcome such attitudes as jealousy, pride, and murmuring.

As David pondered on the blessings he had received from the Good Shepherd, he said, "My brimming cup runs over" (Ps. 23:5, *Amplified*). We have been provided such an abundant life through Jesus Christ. He said, "I came that they may have and enjoy life, and have it in abundance—to the full, till it overflows" (John 10:10, *Amplified*).

As we are fed at His banqueting table and controlled by His Holy Spirit, we are filled to the full until the cup of our lives overflows.

It is not the cup that is important. Cups are made of various kinds of material; some are ordinary earthenware cups, others of lovely china. They are various sizes and for various uses. It is important, however, what we are filled with. Only that with which we are filled overflows. It is important to be in the place of God's choosing so He can channel the overflow for His purpose.

The cup of our lives should be full to overflowing with the life of Jesus Christ Himself.

Someone has said, "Our cup may be small, but we can overflow. We may not hold much, but we can overflow a lot."

Psalm 23:6

Surely goodness and mercy shall follow me all the days of my life: and I will dwell in the house of the Lord for ever.

In David's daily walk with God he learned that his Good Shepherd was sufficient for every need. He could say from his personal experience, "Surely goodness and mercy shall follow me all the days of my life."

As we look ahead we cannot see "all the days of my life" that lie ahead. David said "ALL" the days, January through December; not just the bright days but the dark ones, not only the easy days but the difficult ones. He doesn't say months or years, but "days"—the "days of my life," each one of them.

Do we look ahead and wonder what next year or next

week or tomorrow holds for us? Regardless of what comes, there will never be a day that God's choice guardians, goodness and mercy, will not follow us. They will accompany us every day on our earthly pilgrimage.

They are attributes of God. David wrote, "O taste and see that the Lord is GOOD" (Ps. 34:8). Paul wrote, "But God, who is rich in mercy" (Eph. 2:4).

Someone has said, "Goodness to supply every want, mercy to forgive every sin; goodness to provide, mercy to pardon."

David said, "SURELY goodness and mercy shall follow me." We can be assured of this because He has never failed in the past; because He has pledged His Word and it has never failed. We can have the assurance of knowing that His goodness and mercy are with us today.

It is personal for us, as it was for David. We can say, "shall follow ME all the days of MY life."

When life comes to a close on earth, I can say, "I will dwell in the house of the Lord for ever." Jesus promised, "In my Father's house are many mansions: if it were not so, I would have told you. I go to prepare a place for you. And if I go and prepare a place for you, I will come again, and receive you unto myself; that where I am, there ye may be also" (John 14:2, 3).

Psalm 25:1

Unto thee, O Lord, do I lift up my soul.

David lived in such close fellowship with God that in a moment of need he could instantly lift up his soul to his Heavenly Father. He was on intimate speaking terms with God and kept an open channel between them that his prayers might not be hindered. David approached God in great humility, recognizing the holiness of God and his own unworthiness. Thus he experienced the power of a life of prayer.

As we study the biographies of godly men who through the years have had great influence for God in the world, we discover that their lives have been saturated with prayer. William Hewitson of Dirleton was a great man of God. Dr. Andrew Bonar, who had a very high regard for him, said, "One thing often struck me in Mr. Hewitson. He seemed to have no intervals in communion with God—no gaps. I used to feel, when with him, that it was being with one who was a vine watered every moment. Hewitson could say, 'I am better acquainted with Jesus than with any friend I have on earth.'"

During World War II a British soldier was caught creeping stealthily from a near-by woods to his quarters. He was immediately taken before his commanding officer and charged with communicating with the enemy. His only defense was that he had been praying. The officer demanded, "Are you in the habit of praying?" "Yes, sir," the soldier replied. "Then get down on your knees and pray," his superior ordered. Expecting to be quickly executed, the soldier knelt and poured out his soul in prayer. When he finished the officer said, "You may go. I believe your story. If you hadn't drilled often, you couldn't have done so well in review."

Psalm 25:4, 5

Show me Thy ways, O Lord; teach me Thy paths. Guide me in Thy truth and instruct me: for Thou art the God of my salvation: for Thee I wait all day. (BERKELEY)

Before taking a trip, we study maps and plan our entire route. Then we make more detailed plans and get as much helpful information as we can. As we travel we stop from time to time for further directions and instructions.

God has a plan for each of us as we journey through life. Every one of us needs to pray, "Show me *Thy* ways, O Lord." We may not see a great distance ahead, but He will lead us step by step if we but wait on Him.

David asked God to teach him. Who could be a better teacher than the One who made us and who knows all our ways from the beginning to the very end? In Him is all wisdom and knowledge. The Holy Spirit will reveal God's will to us and make it real in our daily lives as we search the Word and pray.

As we travel through life we need to stop for guidance and direction so that we won't make a wrong turn or lose our way. The Holy Spirit will use the Word, prayer and circumstances, to guide us on our journey through life.

A member of the Salvation Army was faced with a perplexing decision. On a table in a room where he was staying was an open Bible. His attention was captured by this text: "The God of my mercy shall prevenet me." "Prevenet" is an Old English word for "go before." Someone had written in the margin another rendering,

"My God in His loving-kindness shall meet me at every corner." These words assured the man that God would enable him to make the right decision.

We, too, can face the future unafraid, knowing that God will meet us at every corner to show us and guide us in His way.

Psalm 25:14

The secret of the Lord is with them that fear him.

Someone has translated this Scripture verse as, "The friendship of Jehovah is with them that fear Him."

A friend has been defined as, "One who knows all about you and still loves you." I have some close friendships which I cherish very much. These friends have endeared themselves to me. They have shown expressions of their love and friendship. They have been understanding. They have been dependable. They know my faults, yet, because they love me, they overlook them.

What an awesome, humbling truth this—I can have the friendship of Jehovah. All that characterizes a true friendship is exemplified in God's relationship with each of us. "There is a friend that sticketh closer than a brother" (Prov. 18:24). How deeply He loves us. He knows all about us. He loves us just as we are. His love never changes. "Yea, I have loved thee with an everlasting love" (Jer. 31:3). He is always faithful. "Great is THY faithfulness" (Lam. 3:23).

True friends enjoy each other's company and want to spend time together. There are things you confide to your dearest friend, things you couldn't share with anyone else. It is an honor to have a secret entrusted to you.

Our dearest Friend, the Lord Jesus, has special secrets to share with us from His Word and in our times of prayer. This means we must spend time with Him. As our friendship deepens, He can entrust more secrets to us.

Some of His secrets may come in rough wrappings, but within are secret gems from His heart of love.

There must be a response on the part of both parties to keep up a friendship. The Lord is ready to be our "Dearest Friend." Are we responding to His friendship?

We often sing, "What a friend we have in Jesus, all our sins and griefs to bear." WHAT A FRIEND! God desires our friendship, undeserving and unlovely as we are. As we ponder the privilege of friendship with Him, we bow in humbleness. As our heart fills with love for Him, it overflows with His love for us.

"We love him, because he first loved us" (1 John 4:19).

Psalm 27:1

The Lord is my light and my salvation; whom shall I fear? the Lord is the strength of my life; of whom shall I be afraid?

Most of us must confess that we have been fearful at some time in our lives. Fear is a natural emotion, very real in our lives. If we are not careful, it can become a controlling power over us.

But God has promised freedom from fear, for the Lord is our LIGHT, and lightens our path before us step by step.

One dark night we were driving on a desolate road across the desert. No stars could be seen in the sky; the moon was hidden behind the clouds. Suddenly the car lights went out. For a moment fear gripped our hearts, for we could see nothing. Just as suddenly, the lights came on again and the fear was gone.

So in our lives, there are times when the lights go out. We are in complete darkness. We cannot see the way ahead. Fear grips our hearts. But God is with us in the darkness and His presence illuminates our lives. In His own time He shows us the next step ahead for us.

We can also be free from fear for He is our SALVATION. He is the all-powerful one in Whom we put our complete trust, confident that He can lead us safely along His path for us.

Then we can be free from fear for He is our STRENGTH. He is our constant source of power. Could anything be more powerful than our lives plus God, His all-powerfulness in our weakness?

He was our confidence in the past. "When the wicked, even mine enemies and my foes, came [past tense] upon me to eat up my flesh, they stumbled and fell" (Ps. 27:2). He is our confidence for the future. "Though an host should encamp against me, my heart shall [future tense] not fear" (v. 3). He is our confidence all through life. "I sought the Lord, and he heard me, and delivered me from ALL MY FEARS" (Ps. 34:4).

In the light of His presence I shall not fear; in the security of His presence I shall not be afraid.

Psalm 27:4

One thing have I desired of the Lord, that will I seek after; that I may dwell in the house of the Lord all the days of my life, to behold the beauty of the Lord, and to inquire in his temple.

Late for an appointment, a man hurried out and hailed a cab. Jumping in, he said to the driver, "Get going and drive as quickly as you can." After a few blocks, he impatiently asked, "Are we almost there?" "Almost where?" replied the driver. In his hurry the passenger had failed to give the driver the address of his destination.

That may seem an unlikely story, yet today many people are so busy trying to keep up with the rapid pace of living, they haven't stopped to consider what their goal in life is.

David had a goal in his life, a goal that his heart was set on achieving. He said, "ONE THING have I asked of the Lord, that will I seek after" (Ps. 27:4, *Amplified*).

Since David was in danger, helpless, and friendless, he might have prayed for his safety, but that was not the primary desire of his heart.

First, his heart's desire was "that I may dwell in the house of the Lord—in His Presence—all the days of my life." He wanted to live in the presence of the Lord all the days of his life. He longed for the constant companionship of God,

Next, his desire was "to behold the beauty of the Lord." He wanted his vision filled with the Lord.

Then he wanted "to inquire in his temple." He wanted God's answers to his problems; to know God's will; to become better acquainted with God.

He had his priorities right. He longed for companionship with the Lord—to be occupied with God's Person; he wanted to seek His will—to be occupied with God's guidance.

Jesus Christ came that through Him we might have the constant companionship of God, see Him with our eyes of faith, and walk in obedience to His will.

Psalm 27:13

I had fainted, unless I had believed to see the goodness of the Lord in the land of the living.

God encourages us through His Word. In it He gives principles and guidelines for our lives—lives often filled with perplexities, uncertainties, and insecurities.

David experienced many of the same situations we face. Often he was faint of heart, falling into the depths of despair. Discouragement and disappointment were very real to him. He knew what it was to come to the end of himself. He said, "I had fainted."

But David had discovered a key word that changed his spirit of defeat to victory. "I had fainted UNLESS." Unless what? "I had BELIEVED to see the goodness of the Lord in the land of the living." It is often said, "Seeing is believing." But David believed God when he couldn't see the outcome. When he was almost fainting he looked to God, believing Him, trusting Him.

There was a time in my life when I went through deep waters. My husband was ill for many years and for some time he was depressed. Because of the strain of encouraging him and the lack of sleep, I became exhausted. Many times I felt I could not continue another day. Often it seemed I would faint beneath the load. I cried to the Lord day after day, telling Him I had reached the end.

I, too, learned the importance of the word "UNLESS." I would have fainted UNLESS I had learned to "believe to see the goodness of the Lord." I focused my eyes, not on my problem, but on the Lord. Instead of fainting, I experienced the rest that comes from trusting Him completely.

Are you fainting today beneath the load of your care? Do you feel you have reached the end? Instead of fainting, believe God. As you trust Him, your TROUBLES can become TRIUMPHS. It has been said, "God doesn't have problems, He has plans; and He will take our problems and convert them into His plans if we will let Him."

In Isaiah 40:29 we find God's remedy, "He giveth POWER to the FAINT; and to them that have no might he increaseth strength."

Psalm 27:14

Wait on the Lord: be of good courage, and he shall strengthen thine heart: wait, I say, on the Lord.

Today we see turmoil and confusion. There is an alarming increase in crime. The cost of living is rising. Men's hearts today are filled with fear.

Even in David's day there was much to cause fear. He said that he would faint unless he had faith to look away from the condition of the world about him and look to God who made the world and was still in control. He saw the "goodness" of the Lord as the sun rose and set faithfully day after day. He saw the "goodness" of the Lord in nature. This was a reminder of the "goodness" and "faithfulness" of God to His own children. It deepened David's trust in his Heavenly Father.

The psalmist gives the secret of the strength and courage needed to live in such a world—a little four-letter word—"*Wait* on the Lord." The ability to wait is not easily acquired. We are restless and want to be on the move. We do not like to wait in line, or wait in the doctor's office—in fact, most of us just do not like to wait. It is much easier to act than to wait. Someone has said, "Waiting on God is not one of the marks of the average space-age Christian."

Waiting on the Lord is seeking His face for guidance and direction in our lives. It is becoming quiet enough before Him to hear His voice. If we do not take time to wait on Him we may go forth in the energy of the flesh or we may force open a door before His time.

Wait! His clock and His calendar are not always the same as ours, but they are always right on time.

Psalm 28:9

Save thy people, and bless thine inheritance; feed them also, and lift them up for ever.

David was a man of prayer. His prayer life is an example to us and can enrich our prayer lives. He had the joy and peace of a life lived in communion with God. Before making his needs known to God, he took time to hear his Heavenly Father speak to him. "Unto thee will I cry, O Lord my rock; be not silent unto me," he said (v. 1).

After communing with God, he brought his petitions to Him. "Hear the voice of my supplication, when I cry unto thee," he prayed. Sometimes we try everything else before we finally resort to prayer. David had learned from personal experience that God hears and answers prayer. So, too, God wants us to take our needs to Him. David remembered to thank God for answered prayer. Often we forget this. "Blessed be the Lord, because he hath heard the voice of my supplications," he declared gratefully.

David was moved to pray for others also. His heart was tender toward them and their needs. "Save them, bless them, feed them and lift them up," he prayed. He asked God to preserve and keep them. David prayed that God's children might be well nourished. Food is necessary for life. When we do not eat, we become weak. Malnutrition and lowered resistance to disease result from lack of food. The same is true in our spiritual lives. We must be fed if we are to be spiritually strong and well. As we are nourished our spirits are lifted and our strength is renewed. In Psalm 3:3 we read, "But You, O Lord, are a shield for me, my glory, and the lifter up of my head" (*Amplified*).

Communion, petition, intercession—these had a place in David's prayer life. May they have a place in yours also.

Psalm 29:11

The Lord will give strength unto his people; the Lord will bless his people with peace.

A popular song we used to sing is entitled "Stormy Weather." In Psalm 29 David reminds us that we may encounter "stormy weather" experiences in our lives.

During these turbulent times we need a security strong enough to carry us through.

Throughout Psalm 29 one phrase, "the voice of the Lord," is repeated several times. We are told the meaning of the name "Lord" in this Psalm is, "He [who] is."

As the storms come, we can be assured that "He who is" is in them, going through them with us even though we may not see Him.

He allows the storm so that we may learn necessary lessons and so that He may give us opportunities to be brought into a closer walk with Him. Even our obedience to Him may lead us into a storm.

His resources are adequate and His promises sure. He has promised us a limitless supply of strength, a strength equal to our needs. It comes from waiting upon the Lord. "They that wait upon the Lord shall renew their strength" (Isa. 40:31). It is said that as a storm approaches, the eagle is the only bird that will not seek shelter. He faces the storm, and with wings spread, allows the storm to carry him to higher heights. So, as God draws near in the storm, He lifts us by His strength to higher spiritual heights.

Not only are we given strength to go through the

storm, but a tranquil heart and mind in the fury of the storm. The peace He gives is a part of the fruit of the Spirit. It is a supernatural calm produced by the Holy Spirit.

The "God who is" is with us today, with His provision of strength and peace. Why be weak when we have His strength? Why be troubled when we have His peace?

Someone has said, "The strength of the Lord enables us to bear the pressure of the storm; the peace of God keeps the disturbing elements of the outer storm from penetrating our inner being."

Psalm 32:7

Thou art my hiding place; thou shalt preserve me from trouble; thou shalt compass me about with songs of deliverance. Selah.

Songs! Music! What an effect music can have on us. Often when we are depressed or discouraged, the sound of music can lift our spirits, and drive away the feeling of despair. God is the Master Musician and gives songs an important place in our Christian experience.

God had filled David's life with song, giving him a "singing heart." The Psalms are filled with his praises and songs to God. As we study his life, we discover it was not an easy one. He experienced persecution. Several times the king tried to take David's life. Some of his family and close friends became his enemies. But through his trouble he learned to know God who could deliver him from them. In spite of all his heartaches, he could say, "I will bless the Lord at all times: his praise shall continually be in my mouth" (Ps. 34:1).

In Psalm 32:7 he wrote of his songs of deliverance. He could sing in the midst of trouble, for his security was in God who was the "source of his song." He said, "You are my hiding place from every storm of life" (LB). He was not spared from stormy trials, but he was assured of God's protection from the devastating effects of the storms. Sometimes he was protected IN storms; at other times he was protected FROM them. He said, "Thou shalt preserve me from trouble."

No wonder David could sing. He said, "You surround me with SONGS of victory" (LB). Encompassed with songs of deliverance and victory, why shouldn't he sing?

Is your heart a "singing heart" today? Regardless of present pressures, you can have a SONG—a song of deliverance. Someone has said, "It is easy to sing when we can read the notes by daylight. But God enables us to sing where there is not a ray of light to read by."

Our hearts are filled with joy and peace as we are surrounded with His songs of deliverance. "With jubilant songs of deliverance thou wilt surround me."

Psalm 32:8

I will instruct thee and teach thee in the way which thou shalt go: I will guide thee with mine eye.

In preparation for daily living, we enter as a student in God's University. He promises to be our teacher. "I, the Lord" (Ps. 32:8, *Amplified*).

God promises three things in this verse. First, He says, "I will INSTRUCT thee." Instruct means to communicate knowledge, to inform. God will impart to us the knowledge we need to walk in the light of His will. He imparts this knowledge in such a way that we can know and understand. His Book of Instructions is the Bible. It has been said, "When all else fails, read the instructions." We will not always find specific directions, as, "do this" or "don't do that." It would be easier if we did. Yet as we read it regularly our hearts and minds are open to His instruction. He can reveal His will to us.

Next, He says, "I will TEACH you in the way you should go." "I will train you" (*Berkeley*). So God has provided a Practical Training Course and the Holy Spirit is our special Instructor for it. "But the Comforter, which is the Holy Ghost, whom the Father will send in my name, he shall teach you all things, and bring all things to your remembrance, whatsoever I have said unto you" (John 14:26).

Many schools have special counselors who give guidance and direction to the students. God gives special counseling, too. He says, "I will COUNSEL you with My eye upon you" (*Amplified*). God sees our "step-by-step" needs and gives "step-by-step" counseling, for He keeps His eye upon us at all times. "Behold, he that keepeth Israel shall neither slumber nor sleep" (Ps. 121:4).

What a wonderful promise for us in our daily living. Often problems arise that we do not know how to handle. There may be needs with no apparent solution. Situations may be beyond human possibilities. God's promise for you: "I will instruct you—I will teach you—I will counsel you."

Someone has encouraged us by saying, "We are partners with God to do the impossible."

Psalm 33:12

Blessed is the nation whose God is the Lord; and the people whom he hath chosen for his own inheritance.

Our country was founded on its belief in God. In the summer of 1776, delegates from thirteen colonies met to consider the future of the new country. Suggestion after suggestion was offered and rejected. Finally the discouraged delegates turned to Benjamin Franklin for his opinion. Hesitating a moment, he slowly rose and delivered a brief but powerful message based on Psalm 127:1. "Except the Lord build the house, they labour in vain that build it: except the Lord keep the city, the watchman waketh but in vain." He suggested a time of prayer. A spirit of unity resulted and the Declaration of Independence was written. As the Liberty Bell rang for the first time in Independence Hall, it proclaimed the birth of the United States of America on July 4, 1776.

Eighty-seven years later, during a time of great crisis, President Lincoln, in his famous Gettysburg Address, challenged the people of America to resolve "that this nation, under God, shall have a new birth of freedom—and that government of the people, by the people, for the people, shall not perish from the earth." There are forces at work today which are trying to take away this freedom. These enemies are strong. Unless America acknowledges her dependence on God, we could lose this freedom so dear to us.

Prayer has changed the course of history in the past. It is still as powerful today. "If my people, which are called by my name, shall humble themselves, and pray, and seek my face, and turn from their wicked ways; then will I hear from heaven, and will forgive their sin, and will heal their land" (2 Chron. 7:14).

The late President Kennedy, in his inaugural address, said, "Do not ask what your country can do for you, but ask what you can do for your country." *Pray* that our United States of America may continue as a nation "under God."

Psalm 34:1

I will bless the Lord at all times; his praise shall continually be in my mouth.

This is the "All" Psalm. David wrote it when he was a homeless exile. During this time of great trouble in his life, there was seemingly nothing for which to praise God. Yet the psalmist praised God continually.

Can we, like David, praise the Lord at all times? Can we praise Him when sorrow comes? When heartache overwhelms us? Can we praise Him when friends fail us? When we have financial reverses? David said, "I will bless the Lord at *all* times." He could do this because he looked beyond his circumstances to the Lord. He believed the truth of Romans 8:28, "We are assured and know that [God being a partner in their labor] all things work together and are [fitting into a plan] for good to those who love God and are called according to [His] design and purpose" (*Amplified*).

David said, "I sought the Lord, and he heard me, and delivered me from *all* my fears" (v. 4). David was not delivered from some of his fears, or nearly all of them, but from *all* of them, every one. He went to the source of deliverance. He "sought the *Lord,*" the One who could deliver completely. What fears do you have today? The Lord can give you complete deliverance from *all* of them.

David was also delivered from *all* his troubles. "This poor man cried, and the Lord heard him, and saved him out of *all* his troubles"—not merely the great ones, or the small ones, or the majority of them, but from *all* of them. The Lord can do the same for you.

In verse 6 we note the past tense of the verbs—"cried," "heard," and "delivered." In verse 17 they are in the present tense—"cry," "heareth," and "delivereth." He who heard and answered yesterday will do the same today. We must not think that Christians will escape trouble, for we read, "Many are the afflictions of the righteous; *but* the Lord delivereth him out of them *all*" (v. 19). How wonderful to know God, the *all*-sufficient One, and to experience the reality of His complete deliverance as we bring *all* our needs to Him.

Psalm 34:4, 6, 19

I sought the Lord, and he heard me, and delivered me from all fears. . . . This poor man cried, and the Lord heard him, and saved him out of all his troubles. . . . Many are the afflictions of the righteous: but the Lord delivereth him out of them all.

Psalm 34 begins with David praising God. The above verses reveal the reason for his praise. Fear had filled his heart because of the trouble he had been experiencing.

Knowing and believing in the power of prayer, he sought the Lord, his sure source of help.

God heard and delivered him out of ALL his fears, ALL his troubles, ALL his afflictions. No wonder his heart was so full of praise to God!

Fear! Trouble! Affliction! Who has not experienced them? Fear has filled our hearts, troubles have mounted, afflictions have crushed us. What God did for David, He can do for us. If we seek Him, He will hear and deliver. He has promised to deliver us from EVERY trouble, from EVERY affliction.

Deliverance may not come in the way we expect it, or at the time we want it. He may not deliver us out of them all, but He will deliver us in the midst of them all.

In his later years of life, George Frederick Handel lost his money. His health failed. His right side became paralyzed. His creditors were threatening him with imprisonment for non-payment of his debts. He had no place to go but to God. Putting his trust completely in Him to meet his needs, he decided to go into seclusion. There he spent much time in meditation and prayer. Out of this time spent with God came the greatest of all his oratorios, "THE MESSIAH."

Someone has said, "He who knows God and remembers that He has a father's heart and a mother's concern for His own, will never be panic-stricken even when all that is considered stable and permanent comes down with a crash."

"The angel of the Lord encampeth round about them that fear him, and delivereth them" (v. 7).

Psalm 34:5

They looked to Him, and were radiant. (AMPLIFIED)

Some people always seem to radiate joy from their lives. It sparkles from their eyes and bubbles from their lips. Just looking at them gives a lift to our spirits. Through observation we discover that their radiance comes from within. It is as though a light had been turned on in their lives.

The secret of this inner radiance is found in this verse: "They looked unto HIM, and were radiant." The Lord is the source of their radiance. A Chinese version of this verse reads, "All who look to the Lord have light on their faces."

The Lord Jesus said, "I am the light of the world" (John 8:12). As we invite Him into our lives, His light is turned on within us. The radiance of His light within reflects His beauty and loveliness. We become radiant Christians.

One morning I stood chatting with a waitress in a dining room where I was having an early morning breakfast meeting. She said to me, "Look at these women; how happy they are. Look at their smiling faces at eight o'clock in the morning." She was observing the radiance of the presence of Christ in their lives.

This does not mean that radiant Christians are free from trials. But they have taken God into their plans, committed their way to Him, and are looking to Him in restful confidence.

One time when Adoniram Judson was home on

furlough, a boy, seeing him on the street, thought he had never seen such light on a human face. Finally he recognized him as a missionary whose picture he had once seen. The young boy was Henry Clay Trumbull who later became a famous minister himself and wrote a book of memories. One chapter he entitled "What a Boy Saw in the Face of Adoniram Judson."

"But we all, with open face beholding as in a glass the glory of the Lord, are changed into the same image from glory to glory, even as by the Spirit of the Lord" (2 Cor. 3:18).

"There will be more reflection of Jesus when there is more reflection on Him."

Psalm 34:8

O taste and see that the Lord is good.

When something wonderful happens to us, we say, "The Lord is so good." But what happens when trouble comes, when health fails, when we lose our job, when our homes fall apart? What about the times our hearts are crushed with sorrow, our bodies suffer pain, we are misunderstood? Do we still say, "The Lord is good"?

When difficulties come, the enemy of our soul will try to cause us to doubt the goodness of the Lord. But we must remember that He is always good. He is just as good in the dark times as when everything is going smoothly.

David speaks in Psalm 34, not from a problem-free life, but from one filled with trouble, with heartache, with sorrow. But through it all he had made a great discovery. "The LORD is good." He encourages us to make this same discovery: "Taste and see that HE IS good."

Taste is defined as "to sample, test, experience." David encourages us to "sample" or to "taste," that we might see that the Lord is good. As we begin "sampling" the Word of God, a desire is created for more of the Lord. Jeremiah wrote, "Thy words were found, and I did eat them; and thy word was unto me the joy and rejoicing of mine heart" (Jer. 15:16).

Taste also means "test." As we put His promises to the test, claiming them for our need, we learn that the Lord who keeps His promises is good.

Taste has another meaning, "experience." As we put Him to the test in our lives, He becomes increasingly real in our life experience. There we learn that God is good in every circumstance of our lives.

If David were here today, he would say, "Taste and see for yourself that the Lord is good." As we taste, sample, test, and experience Him, we discover that He is good. When we believe He is ALWAYS good, it gives us confidence and security.

"Oh that men would praise the Lord for his goodness, and for his wonderful works to the children of men" (Ps. 107:8).

Psalm 36:7

How excellent is thy lovingkindness, O God! therefore the children of men put their trust under the shadow of thy wings.

In this Psalm, David shares a cluster of precious gems with those who have experienced the "steadfast love" of God (Ps. 36:5, LB).

Lovingkindness is described as "love in action." God's lovingkindness is His love put into action, which He demonstrated by sending the Lord Jesus to earth. "But God showed his great love for us by sending Christ to die for us while we were still sinners" (Rom. 5:8, LB).

First, there is safety for God's children. "Therefore the children of men put their trust under the shadow of thy wings." Even in times of great danger we are guaranteed a place of safety. He that "putteth his trust in the Lord shall be safe" (Prov. 29:25).

In Him we have adequate provisions. "They shall be abundantly satisfied with the fatness of thy house" (Ps. 36:8). Do we live meagerly when we could be partaking of His abundant supplies?

He not only gives us the capacity to drink "of the rivers of His pleasure," but causes us to drink. "I will make them to drink."

God is the source of our life: "with thee is the fountain of life" (v. 9). As we bring our needs and hold them under His unfailing fountain, He fills them from His resources.

Our way may be dark about us, but He is light, and "in thy light we see light."

One time a husband bought a match box for his wife. It was supposed to glow in the dark. But it didn't. The husband thought he had been cheated. Then he discovered some French words on the box. When translated it read, "If you want me to shine in the night, keep me in the sunlight through the day."

As we spend time in His presence, we absorb the rays of the Light of His Word. Then when our way is dark, the light of His presence shines on our path.

These precious gems from His Word reveal the lovingkindness of God. Are they yours?

Psalm 37:4

Delight thyself also in the Lord; and he shall give thee the desires of thine heart.

As you read this promise are you tempted to say, "This is not true in my life. Instead of receiving my desires, it seems that even what I have is being taken away from me. It may work for others but not for me"?

God has promised to give us the desires of our heart, but there is a condition to be fulfilled—we are to "delight thyself in the LORD." We often hurry over the first part of this verse and concern ourselves with the promise of receiving our desires. Yet to have our desires we must be on receiving ground—"delighting in Him."

We are to delight in His Word. "Thy Word was unto me the joy and rejoicing of mine heart" (Jer. 15:16). And we are to delight in His will. "I delight to do thy will, O my God" (Ps. 40:8). Also, we are to delight in His presence. "In thy presence is fullness of joy; at thy right hand there are pleasures for evermore" (Ps. 16:11).

In what are we delighting today? Our homes? Our families? Our social life? Our business? God tells us to delight in Him if we want Him to give us our desires. By delighting in Him we find that our desires are to please Him. These other things can be enjoyed if we have Him in His rightful place.

Someone has said, "The more we delight in Him, the less we will desire things." The source of our delight is the secret of receiving our desires.

Psalm 37:5

Commit your way to the Lord—roll and repose [each care of] your road on Him; trust, lean on, rely on and be confident also in Him, and He will bring it to pass. (AMPLIFIED)

Do you face insurmountable problems? Does there seem to be no solution? God says, "Commit and trust and I will bring it to pass." This is a conditional promise. He will work in our behalf *if* we commit and trust.

The word "commit" has several meanings: "to entrust"; "to hand over to someone else"; "to let go so another can take over." Once I heard this illustration of committal. When we mail a letter, we have confidence that the Post Office Department will deliver it to the person to whom it is addressed. However, the letter cannot be delivered until we "let go" and drop it into the mailbox.

What need do you have? What problem? There is not one too great or too small to bring to God. He is saying, "Hand it over to Me; trust Me with it." Drop it into God's Mailbox, take your hands off completely and let Him work.

A literal translation can read, "Roll upon Jehovah thy way; trust upon Him; and He worketh." When our burdens seem too heavy to lift, we can roll them on Him. Then He *works;* the meaning is not "will work" but "is working now." Someone has said, "*Relinquish* and *rest;* then leave the *results* with Him."

A pilot, lost in the clouds and fog, was not experienced

in instrument landing. The station tower promised to bring him in on radar. He began to receive his instructions when suddenly he remembered a tall pole which was in the flight path. Frantically he called the tower. The command came back, "You obey the *instructions:* we will take care of the *obstructions.*"

We may be in a fog. The clouds of trouble may be heavy above us. We may be looking only at the obstacles before us. God says, "You are to obey My instructions [commit and trust]; I will take care of the obstructions [and bring it to pass]."

Psalm 37:7

Rest in the Lord, and wait patiently for him.

Many people seem to get up as tired as when they went to bed. Much of this weariness is caused by the pressures of life and a lack of rest in the inner man.

Rest is necessary for the body and the mind. There is a great need, too, for rest within. This Psalm mentions several steps which lead to this inner rest: "Fret not" (v. 1); "Trust in the Lord" (v. 3); "Delight thyself also in the Lord" (v. 4); "Commit thy way unto the Lord" (v. 5).

The source of this rest is in the Lord. Instead of being irritable, and fuming and fussing, we can have the inner quietness of resting "in the Lord." This is a rest we can possess even in the midst of ceaseless activity. A. B. Simpson speaks of "rested workers." He said, "There is an energy that may be tireless and ceaseless and yet still as the ocean depths."

Perhaps you are faced with a particularly busy day at

home. The telephone rings—someone needs a word of comfort. Later a friend comes with a problem to discuss. About that time one of the children is hurt and demands attention. Or perhaps you have an exceptionally busy day at the office. In the midst of it a customer comes in with a complaint that you must satisfy. Then you are asked to do some extra work which must be completed immediately.

Such interruptions can upset and annoy us. Yet we can have a quietness in the midst of these irritations. We can "rest in the Lord." Accept the day with its changes as from Him. Instead of becoming irritable, thank Him for the changed schedule and say, "My times are in thy hand" (Ps. 31:15).

Psalm 37:23

The steps of a [good] man are directed and established of the Lord, when He delights in his way [and He busies Himself with his every step]. (AMPLIFIED)

Walking is a common everyday experience. It is so much a part of life that we give little thought to it. How many steps do you think you take each day?

There is a Chinese proverb that says, "A journey of a thousand miles begins with just one step." Our life of faith is a step-by-step journey.

The above verse tells us that "the steps of a [good] man are directed . . . of the Lord." This doesn't imply that we are good; in ourselves we cannot qualify. None of us are good enough to meet God's perfect standard. But He has made it possible for us to be "good" through our personal faith in Jesus Christ as Savior. He is our "righteousness" or our "goodness."

God delights to direct the steps of His own children. Sometimes He turns on the "green go-light," giving us a clear direction to go ahead. At other times we see the "red stop-light." We then have to wait until the light changes again. He controls the switches and knows when to turn on the one and turn off the other. "The *stops* of a good man are ordered by the Lord as well as his steps."

God busies Himself with every one of our steps. How tenderly and lovingly parents watch over their children! They reach out a hand to keep them from stumbling and they lift them up if they fall. All through our lives God busies Himself with us, lifting us up if we fall, encouraging and strengthening us along the way.

It has been said, "I know not the way He leads me, but well do I know my Guide."

Psalm 40:3

And he hath put a new song in my mouth, even praise unto our God.

One of the lovely gospel songs we sing is "Praise Him! Praise Him! Jesus our blessed redeemer. Sing O earth, His wonderful love proclaim." Praise is glorifying God; being occupied with His blessings. Many are the blessings for which we can praise Him.

Sometimes we think it takes pleasant, quiet surroundings in our lives to give us a song of praise. But David had learned the blessing of praising Him in the time of trouble and danger. When in a precarious position, completely helpless in a deep pit and struggling in the miry clay, he went into God's presence and poured out his heart. As he waited patiently and expectantly, God heard his cry and answered.

David said, "He drew me up out of a horrible pit—a pit of tumult and of destruction—out of the miry clay, froth and slime, and set my feet upon a rock, steadying my steps and establishing my goings" (Ps. 40:2, *Amplified*).

Then God gave him a "singing heart," a heart filled with praise. God had lifted him from his insecure and slippery position to a place of security on a rock. No wonder he could praise God. In Psalm 34:1 he said, "I will bless the Lord at all times: HIS PRAISE shall continually be in my mouth."

God has done this same thing for us. From the depths of sin, He lifted us and set us upon the Rock. The rock symbolizes Christ, the Rock of our salvation, our Source of security and strength.

Then He gave us a new song, one which continues throughout our lives. It is a song of praise for what He has done for us, and continues to do. Each new trial brings a new song of praise. Each new answer to prayer gives new opportunities to praise God, the One who is both the source and object of our song.

May we let God give us a NEW SONG of PRAISE today whatever our circumstances may be. "Many shall see it, and fear, and shall trust in the Lord" (Ps. 40:3).

Psalm 42:1, 2

As the hart pants and longs for the water brooks, so I pant and long for you, O God. My inner self thirsts for God, for the living God. When shall I come and behold the face of God? (AMPLIFIED)

The writer of this Psalm tells of the longing of his innermost being for God. He uses the illustration of a deer craving water to quench its thirst, perhaps after having been pursued almost to the point of exhaustion. As the deer craves water, so the soul thirsts after God.

Someone has called this Scripture passage, "The Pursuit of God." The heart of man is created in such a way by God that we are incomplete until He occupies His rightful place in our lives. Augustine said, "Thou hast made us for thyself, O God, and our hearts are restless till they find rest in thee." The desire of the writer of this Psalm was not for pleasures, people, or position, for they do not quench the inner thirst of the heart. Only God can do this. His desire was for a new and deeper awareness of the reality of God Himself in his life.

God allows circumstances to come that create a longing in our hearts for Him. The dark times and trials of life, when God seems so far away, can develop a greater hunger and thirst after His presence. As the longing of the heart is satisfied by God's presence, there will be the satisfaction of contentment in Him.

This cry was voiced in Psalm 73:25. "Whom have I in heaven but THEE? And there is none upon earth that I desire beside thee." His heart had complete satisfaction in the Lord.

What is the desire of your heart today? Are you long-ing for a closer walk with Him? Does your innermost being cry out for the reality of God Himself? Sometimes we stop at the blessings and experiences, so we miss the Blesser. The blessings and experiences should lead us to God Himself. As we drink deeply of the Water of Life, our thirst will be quenched and we will be completely satisfied with Him.

"There is NONE upon earth that I desire but THEE."

Psalm 46:1

God is our refuge and strength, a very present help in trouble.

This is a Psalm of comfort and trust for a life filled with trouble. When problems arise and discouragements come, when there is no human source of help, we have the promise that God is "our refuge," "our strength," and "our help."

Refuge is defined as "shelter from danger or distress." The Lord Jesus Christ IS our refuge today (present tense). Hidden in the hollow of His all-mighty hand, we have a shelter that is safe and secure. This refuge is not a place where we escape from the situations and circum-stances of life, but is a protection for us in the midst of them.

Not only is the Lord our refuge in time of trouble, but our strength to endure it. When we realize our limited strength is not sufficient, we discover He has a never-ending supply of strength on which we can draw. "And as thy days, so shall thy strength be" (Deut. 33:25).

He is also our help in trouble. Whatever our need may

be, He wants us to know that, "I AM, right now, this very moment, not only your help in trouble, but a PRESENT help." It has been said, "It sometimes takes trouble for God to get our attention."

When we become Christians, we often assume our days of trouble are over. Soon we discover this is not true. God has a purpose to accomplish through difficulties in our lives. Some lessons can only be learned through trouble.

We are proved and tested in this way. "A very present and WELL-PROVED HELP in trouble" (Ps. 46:1, *Amplified*). "A TESTED help in times of trouble" (LB). It has been said, "Trouble is His vote of confidence in us."

He is a "well-proved help," a "tested help." Are you testing and proving Him as your own personal refuge, strength, and help in your problems and trials of today?

There is a poem that begins, "He's helping me now, this moment; in ways that I know and I know not." He is our help today, whatever our day.

Psalm 46:10

Be still. . . .

We are living in a technological age geared to speed. Speed records are being set in travel enabling us to circle the globe in an unbelievably short time. This accelerated tempo is experienced in every area of living today. A twenty-four hour day is insufficient time to complete all we have scheduled on our calendars. We are always in a hurry, rushing from one thing to another. It is no wonder that tensions build up almost to the breaking point.

We keep stereo, radio, and television on because we cannot stand the stillness. It is as if we are on a carousel revolving so rapidly we cannot get off.

Our Scripture verse for today says, "Be still, and KNOW that I am God." Ask yourself, "How well do I know God? How real is He to me? Is He only a casual acquaintance, or a dear, intimate friend?" Perhaps our greatest need is to deepen our friendship with Him. This will mean spending time with Him. The more time we spend with a person, the better we get to know him. We need a quiet time, a "Be Still" time, each day, alone with the Lord, to become better acquainted.

It is not easy to be perfectly still in God's presence. The harder we try, the more difficult it becomes. We remember something we have forgotten to do. The phone rings. The noise of the world about us becomes louder and louder. Yet times of quiet are necessary for our spiritual well-being. Dr. Gilbert Little, a Christian psychiatrist, was asked for a simple rule for mental health. He answered, "Be still, and know that I am God." Rest is not only important for our physical life, but for our spiritual life, too.

The world says, "Be active; be busy; be industrious." But God says, "BE STILL—be quiet; don't rush." This is not just a cessation of activities, but a quietness of heart and spirit in which we are aware of His presence. In the center of our soul is a place where God dwells, and where, if we enter and close out every other sound, He will speak to us. Someone has said, "It is not in the college or academy, but in the silence of the soul, that we learn the greater lessons of life—and quiet hearts are rare." Many times we do all the talking instead of being quiet enough to listen to Him.

As we continue to wait before Him, the sounds about

us fade away; and we are aware of being in the quietness of His Holy Presence.

In 1 Kings 19:11 and 12, we read that it was not in the wind, nor the earthquake, nor the fire that God spoke to Elijah, but in a still small voice. It is in the stillness of the soul that God speaks to us.

May we take time to be still before Him so we may get to KNOW HIM in a more personal and real way. Be still and reduce self-activity; be still and quit rushing about.

"BE STILL. And know that I AM GOD."

Psalm 46:10

. . . and know that I am God.

One day a little girl slipped into her father's study. Without saying a word, she quietly sat on the floor close beside him, watching him at work. After a while he said, "Honey, is there something you want?" "No," she replied, "I am just sitting here loving you." Soon she left as quietly as she had come in. Little did she know the lesson she had taught her father. She had not come to ask him for anything. She had just wanted to be near him and love him. The thought came to him, "How often do I spend time in God's presence, just loving Him and becoming acquainted with Him? Or do I only come to Him when I have a request to ask of Him?"

God not only wants us to bring our requests to Him, but He also wants us to spend time with Him. Yet we are so busy and have so many needs that we often rush into His presence, make our requests known, and rush out again without taking time to be quiet enough to hear

Him. God says, "Be still, and KNOW THAT I AM GOD."

It has been said, "Quietness is not just the opposite of noise. It is not the absence of excitement, haste, and confusion. These dissipate strength while calmness conserves it. The world's mighty men have grown in solitude." As we study the lives of many Bible characters, we discover that they had a close friendship and walk with God. God spoke of Abraham as "My friend" (Isa. 41:8). David was known as "a man after mine own heart" (Acts 13:22). In reading about the lives of Christians through the ages who were strong in their faith, we learn that they took time to BE STILL and become intimately acquainted with God.

Suppose each of us would pause and make a list of people that we know. What a long list of names we would have! Some we know only by name. Others we recognize by sight. Some are just casual speaking acquaintances. Then there are others who are very dear, intimate friends. We know their likes and dislikes. We enjoy their company. They know all about us and love us just as we are.

In which group of friends is Jesus classified in your life? Is He just a casual acquaintance, or a dear, close friend with whom you enjoy spending time?

Jesus Christ came that He might reveal God to us. "It is true that no one has ever seen God at any time. Yet the divine and only Son, who lives in the closest intimacy with the Father, has made him known" (John 1:18, *Phillips*).

To become better acquainted with God necessitates spending time with Him. It means more than hurriedly reading a verse or two of Scripture and quickly asking God to bless us. We need to enter our spiritual closet, close the door, and become quiet in His presence, meditating on who He is and what He has done for us.

As we become quiet before Him, He can begin to speak and reveal Himself to us. He may say, "Be still and know that I am the all-powerful God. Your need today is not too hard for Me or beyond My power." Or, "Be still and know that I love you. I know all about you, your weaknesses, failures, and mistakes; but I still love you. And My love is stedfast and unchanging." Or, "Be still and know that I am interested in every detail of your life. I want to enter into every need you have—even the need you have today." As we ponder on His greatness and His holiness, yet realize that His love and concern for each of us is very personal, our hearts are filled with worship and adoration.

Often we become so involved in the fast pace of life that we fail to take the necessary time for such fellowship with Him. How well do you know God?

May the prayer of our hearts be that we will take time to "Be still, and KNOW GOD."

Psalm 50:15

And call upon me in the day of trouble; I will deliver thee, and thou shalt glorify me.

When doctors practice together, they usually take turns being "on call" evenings, weekends, and holidays. When patients call, they are referred to the particular doctor on duty.

God has a communication system between Himself and His children. He is always "on call," twenty-four hours a day. Regardless of the number of calls He receives, even many at the same time, He never misses one. He answers each one personally.

Trouble comes to all of us. "Yet man is born unto trouble, as the sparks fly upward" (Job 5:7). It may strike very suddenly. But God is personally "on call." "Call upon Me in YOUR day of trouble." He hears even our weakest cry.

God has given His promise that when we call He will deliver. He doesn't say, "I may deliver," "I will try to deliver," "Perhaps I will deliver," "I will deliver if I feel like it," or "If I'm not too busy I will deliver," but "I WILL deliver."

He who promised to deliver, has the power to do it. "That power belongeth unto God" (Ps. 62:11). He will shake heaven and earth to deliver you if need be. God is the One who delivers, not people, although He often uses people.

What do we do when trouble comes? Do we try every human resource first? All we need do in the midst of trouble is call, and He is on the other end of the line. He assures us He will deliver, but He will do it in a way that will glorify Himself. He promises to deliver us, but He doesn't say when. It may be today, next week, or next year. He is not in a hurry, as we are. He knows the right moment.

After God listens to our need, He completes our call; He delivers us. Sometimes we are delivered from trouble. Sometimes we are delivered from defeat in the midst of trouble. Spurgeon said, "He has solemnly promised, and He will fully perform."

Today we are as close to God as a call. "Call unto ME—and I will deliver THEE."

Psalm 55:6

And I said, Oh that I had wings like a dove! for then would I fly away, and be at rest.

This cry which came from the heart of David the Psalmist is duplicated in the hearts of many in the present day. This is a day of tranquilizers and sleeping pills. To escape the pressures of life and to experience rest is the great quest of people today.

Man was made for God's pleasure and only as God fills His rightful place is a person at rest.

David endured great misunderstandings. Friends and family became his enemies. Into his heart crept a longing to rise up on wings as a dove and fly away from all his troubles and find rest.

Perhaps today you, too, may desire to fly away from your circumstances. Even though the dove is swift in its flight, its wings could never bear us away from life. Though we might be able to leave some situations, we can never get away from ourselves. We are to use our wings not to fly away, but up. The wings of faith will carry us up into the very presence of God where the soul is at rest. Our rest comes only as we are resting in God Himself.

One day someone was watching two birds. One bird was flapping its wings energetically, working hard at it. The other flapped its wings a bit as it rose into the air current, stretched its wings and sailed along with the current.

On wings of faith we can stretch our wings and rise

above the problems of life. Instead of working so hard against the wind currents, we can turn and sail along on the current of His will. Rest then will be ours, rest *in the Lord*.

"Rest in the Lord, and wait patiently for him" (Ps. 37:7).

Psalm 55:17

Evening, and morning, and at noon, will I pray, and cry aloud: and he shall hear my voice.

David knew God, for he spent much time with Him. F. B. Meyer said, "Blessed is the one who retires from the hubbub of the street as did David and Daniel, three times a day."

We are careful to eat three times a day. Shouldn't we pray as often as we eat? God's availability is constant. David didn't pray only when a need arose. He didn't pray merely on the days when he felt like praying. He had regular prayer times.

Constant prayer should be the occupation of the believer. We are not limited to one time and one place. There is no limit to the time we can spend on our knees. What a comfort in these trying days to know that evening, morning, and noon we have entrance into the presence of One whose ear is open to us and who is sensitive to our needs.

Christians everywhere have experienced the strength derived from a constant and instant access into God's holy presence through prayer. I read that someone once asked John Charles Thomas, the famous singer, to what or to whom he owed his success. He quickly replied, "God." He was the son of a minister, and his Christian training profoundly influenced his musical career. Before a concert he would sometimes spend as much as thirty minutes in prayer that God might use his voice to bless others.

Psalm 55:22

Cast thy burden upon the Lord, and he shall sustain thee: he shall never suffer the righteous to be moved.

How often we see someone who looks as if he is carrying the weight of the world on his shoulders. Perhaps at some time someone has said to you, "You look as if you've lost your last friend." Have you ever felt that no one really cared and that you were carrying the burdens of the whole world? In these days of confusion and frustration, such a feeling is a frequent experience. Burdens become increasingly heavy; cares press upon us; problems arise in the home; difficult situations distress us at work; heartaches and sorrows overwhelm us. Are you feeling the weight of these burdens today? Are you facing insurmountable problems for which you have no solution?

God says, "Cast your burdens on *Me*." Often we take our burdens to everyone else before we take them to the Lord. A well-known Gospel song reminds us to take our burdens to the Lord and *leave* them there. When we take our burdens to Him, we are strengthened by His sustaining hand, we are comforted by Him, and we find that He is the One who can solve our problems and lighten our burdens.

Our experiences in life become steppingstones to bring us closer to Him if we let Him carry our burdens. A biologist relates that he was fascinated by an ant carrying a piece of straw which seemed to be a tremendous burden for the tiny insect. The ant came to a small hole which it could not cross. It stopped for a few seconds, and then, with amazing intelligence, used the piece of straw as a bridge over the hole. Learning from this wise little insect, we, too, can use our afflictions as steppingstones.

If we cast our burdens on Him, and slip our hands into His, our adversities are transformed into victories. Someone has said, "Out of the brass of trials God fashions trumpets of triumph."

Psalm 56:3

What time I am afraid, I will trust in thee.

David was always honest in his reactions to the circumstances of his life. He was willing to admit his weaknesses but he didn't concentrate on them. He took them to God and let Him meet them for him.

Fear was very real in his life. He didn't try to cover it, but confessed it. "What time I am afraid."

Today many fears fill our lives. We fear poverty, sickness, loneliness, death. We fear the dangers of the night and the pressures of the day.

David learned that the only way to be released from fears was to TRUST in the Lord. "What time I am afraid, I will trust in thee." He changed the focus of his eyes from his situation to the Lord. Faith replaced fear. He PUT his trust in the Lord. This was an act of his will. "In

God have I put my trust: I will not be afraid what man can do unto me" (Ps. 56:11).

Freedom from fear is the result of confidence and trust in God. We may be helpless against fear, but God is not. When trusting God, there is nothing to fear.

Faith is more than believing what God can do. It is trust in the Person of God Himself. "But without faith it is impossible to please him: for he that cometh to God must believe that he IS, and that he is a rewarder of them that diligently seek him" (Heb. 11:6).

When a person trusts God, he will not be afraid. "I will trust and not be afraid, for the Lord is my strength and song; He is my salvation" (Isa. 12:2, LB).

One day a father discovered his little boy had climbed an old tree. The limbs were beginning to break under the boy's weight. The father held up his arms and called, "Jump! I'll catch you." The little son considered the offer for a moment. Then, as more limbs began to break, he said, "Shall I let go of everything, Daddy, and trust you?"

What a lesson for us. Our heavenly Father wants us to let go of everything and trust Him.

Psalm 56:18

You have seen me tossing and turning through the night. You have collected all my tears and preserved them in your bottle! You have recorded every one in your book. (LB)

Are you an individual who has difficulty sleeping at night? The harder you try, the more you toss and turn. Sometimes our wakefulness is caused by sorrow, pain, or heartache. During the dark night hours the tears fall. Our hearts may be broken. Loneliness may overwhelm us.

David knew what it was to shed tears. "You have seen me tossing and turning during the night. You have collected all my tears and preserved them in your bottle." We read that in Persia and Egypt, tears were sometimes wiped from the eyes and cheeks of a mourner and preserved in a tear bottle. Often a person's tear bottle was buried with him. David asked God to preserve his tears in a bottle and record them in His book.

Sometimes a child will cry over a broken toy. As the parent mends it and returns it to the child, a smile breaks through the tears. Sometimes, however, it is broken beyond repair. Then the parent has to become a special comforter, for the toy will have to be replaced with something else.

Sometimes our tears come from a broken heart. God mends it, and we smile again through our tears. But sometimes God knows that for our own good He must remove something from our lives, something we may consider very dear. The tears may fall; we may not understand why, yet He does it for our good. However, He never removes anything from our lives without replacing it with something else. It has been said, "Our broken things lead us to His better things." God comforts as no one else does. He understands as no one else does.

A time is coming when all tears will be wiped from our eyes. One of these days, we will go to live with Him eternally. "And God shall wipe away ALL tears from their eyes; and there shall be no more death, neither sorrow, nor crying, neither shall there be any more pain: for the former things are passed away" (Rev. 21:4).

Psalm 57:7

My heart is fixed, O God; my heart is steadfast and confident! I will sing and make melody. (AMPLIFIED)

David was being pursued by King Saul. Life was uncertain and insecure for the psalmist. Yet he had *perfect security*. He said, "My soul takes refuge and finds shelter and confidence in You; yes, in the shadow of Your wings will I take refuge and be confident until calamities and destructive storms are passed" (v. 1, *Amplified*). God was his refuge and he was protected by His sheltering wings.

David had perfect security because he knew that God was able to perform all things for him. He declared confidently, "I will cry to God Most High, Who performs on my behalf and rewards me—Who brings to pass [His purposes] for me and surely completes them!" (v. 2, *Amplified*). We have perfect security today in the midst of calamities when we take refuge in God and rest under His sheltering wings. Knowing that our Heavenly Father is able to perform *all things* for us, we are perfectly secure. The expression "all things" (v. 2) means exactly that.

David also had *permanent stability*. One whose security is in God can be steadfast and unmovable at all times and in any situation. When life seems to crash in upon the Christian, he can say, "My soul is bowed down, but my heart is fixed."

Perfect security and permanent stability gave the psalmist a *precious song of victory*. David had a song in the midst of the storm. "I will sing and make melody," he said. It is easy to sing when the days are bright, but a steadfast heart can sing also in times of trouble. A fixed heart has a God-given song in the dark days.

A famous old violin-maker always made his instruments out of wood from the north side of the tree. Why? Because the wood which had endured the brunt of the fierce wind, the icy snow, and the raging storm, gave finer tone to the violin. So trouble and sorrow give to the soul its sweetest melodies.

Psalm 61:2

When my heart is overwhelmed: lead me to the rock that is higher than I.

This Psalm was the cry of David's heart when he was fleeing from his son who was trying to usurp his throne.

His heart heavy with sorrow, he cried to the One who could meet his need. "Hear my cry, O God" (Ps. 61:1). Immediately he had an audience with the King of kings. He continued, "Attend unto my prayer."

When he was almost overwhelmed, with the waves of trouble rolling over him, he said, "From the end of the earth will I cry unto thee, when my heart is overwhelmed: lead me to the rock that is higher than I" (v. 2).

This is the cry from many hearts today. As the storms of life sweep over us we cry, "Lord, hear me: Lord, lead me to the Great Rock of Safety, Jesus Christ Himself."

I recall a day when my life was overwhelmed in the midst of a storm. I felt myself almost sinking under the fury of it. I received a card from a friend that day. She related how she had felt constrained to send me a verse of Scripture. It arrived on the day I desperately needed it and it was this verse in the Psalms. God's timing was so perfect. He used it that day to remind me that He was with me in my storm and that He was allowing it to teach me some new lessons I needed to learn.

He gave me the assurance that He was lifting me above my circumstances to a place of safety and strength in Himself.

When troubles come, we can cry, "Lord, hear me! Lord, lead me." Our storms can become a time of victory as we let Him lift us up to the Rock that is above our storms, our Rock of Safety, Christ Jesus.

Is your heart overwhelmed today? Let Him lift you up to your place of security in that Rock, Christ Jesus.

Psalm 62:1, 5

For God alone my soul waits in silence; from Him comes my salvation. . . . My soul, wait only upon God and silently submit to Him; for my hope and expectation are from Him. (AMPLIFIED)

David's life was filled with trouble, discouragement and heartache. Friends and family had turned against him. Even his life was in danger. He knew what it was to have enemies. But he also knew God and had learned to wait only upon Him.

What do we do when burdens press in upon us? To whom do we go? Sometimes we try to work out the answer ourselves or we go to another person. We go to God only when all else has failed. We need to do what David learned to do—we must wait *only* upon God.

We are to wait "in silence" (v. 1, *Amplified*) and to

"silently submit to Him" (v. 5, *Amplified*). A literal translation is, "Only on God wait thou all hushed, my soul." We are to wait in silence before Him that we might be aware of His holiness and majesty. We need to be still in His presence that we might worship Him for who He is and what He has done. In the hustle and bustle of living we often rush into His holy presence and out again without pausing to wait on Him. We do not take time to tune our souls to Him.

Several missionaries had to make a trek into the bush country. They secured the services of several native guides. The first few days they traveled long hours. One morning the missionaries discovered that the guides had made no preparation for the day's journey and refused to move. When asked why they would not travel that day, the guides answered, "Our souls must catch up with our bodies."

Psalm 62:8

Trust in him at all times; ye people, pour out your heart before him: God is a refuge for us. Selah.

This Psalm is often called the "only" Psalm. The word "only" occurs in it eight times. "Truly" here has the meaning of "only." "My soul, wait thou *only* upon God; for my expectation is from him" (Ps. 62:5). "He *only* is my rock and my salvation: he is my defence; I shall not be moved" (v. 6). Our trust is to be in God and Him *only*.

If you were to count the people in whom you have implicit confidence, those whom you can trust at all times, how many would there be? We can trust God always, at *all* times. He will *never* fail us. We can trust Him when we lose our money, when our health fails, when our families forsake us, when we face trouble and sorrow.

Because we have complete confidence in Him, we can go to Him with every need and pour out our hearts before Him. There are few people with whom we feel free to do this. But He understands as no one else can, and He sympathizes and cares. "It is better to trust in the Lord than to put confidence in man" (Ps. 118:8). How it comforts our hearts to know that we can go to Him and tell Him our innermost needs, knowing that He is a safe refuge for us!

This verse ends with the word "Selah," which means "pause, and think of that; stop, and consider what God is saying."

Psalm 63:1

O God, thou art my God; early will I seek thee: my soul thirsteth for thee, my flesh longeth for thee in a dry and thirsty land, where no water is.

While David was alone in the wilderness he was evidently reminiscing of the time when God had been very real to him in the sanctuary. He still desired the reality of God's presence that he had known in the past. He said, "O God, thou art MY God." From the depths of his soul he cried out, "My soul thirsteth for THEE, my flesh longeth for THEE in a dry and thirsty land, where no water is."

The story is told of a Thai man who came to a Thailand mission station. They said to him, "Are you looking for some medicine?" "No," he replied, "I am looking for God."

There are many hungers and thirsts in the world today. Some people hunger for position; some for power. Others hunger for pleasure, love, or acceptance. People are searching everywhere for things that will satisfy. But inner satisfaction does not come through things. Jesus assures us that the hunger and thirst of our soul can be satisfied. "Blessed are they which do hunger and thirst after righteousness: for they shall be filled" (Matt. 5:6).

Inner fulfillment comes from HIM. David said, "Early will I seek HIM." When we read the Bible we must seek Him on its pages. When we enter the prayer closet we must become quiet enough to hear Him speak to us. We must not stop short of anything less than God Himself.

Today, are you seeking for inner peace? Are you longing for something to satisfy? You can be satisfied; you can have inner fulfillment as you seek and find it in Jesus Christ. He said, "If any man thirst, let him come unto me, and drink" (John 7:37).

Tell HIM today of the longing of your heart. Seek Him from the Word of God. Talk to Him, and let Him talk to you in prayer.

Your inner longing can be satisfied in Him today. "My soul shall be satisfied as with marrow and fatness" (Ps. 63:5).

To see thy power and thy glory, so as I have seen thee in the sanctuary.

David was alone in the wilderness when he prayed this prayer. Yet even though he was lonely, he didn't feel sorry for himself. Someone has said that although he was in the wilderness, there was no wilderness in his heart. He let his thoughts wander back to the time when God had been real to him in the sanctuary.

Now he wanted a fresh revelation of God. It is wonderful to remember what God has done in the past, but it should challenge us to experience God's power and glory in a fresh way today. What has He said to you TODAY? What is He doing for you NOW?

God's power is available for our every need. Paul wrote, "I pray that you will begin to understand how incredibly great HIS POWER is to help those who believe Him" (Eph. 1:19, LB).

His power to work in us goes beyond what we can ask or think. "Now to Him Who, by (in consequence of) the [action of His] power that is at work within us, is able to [carry out His purpose and] do superabundantly, far over and above all that we [dare] ask or think—infinitely beyond our highest prayers, desires, thoughts, hopes or dreams" (Eph. 3:20, *Amplified*).

Charles Ryrie has said, "The glory of God is displaying God to the world." This He did in His Son, Jesus Christ. "And the Word was made flesh, and dwelt among us, (and we beheld his glory, the glory as of the only begotten of the father,) full of grace and truth" (John 1:14).

Today we can see the glory of God revealed to us in Jesus Christ. "God, who first ordered light to shine in darkness, has flooded our hearts with His light, so that we can enlighten men with the knowledge of the glory of God, as we see it in the face of Christ" (2 Cor. 4:6, *Phillips*).

Then as our vision is filled with Him, we can reveal His glory to others wherever we may go.

Psalm 63:6

When I remember thee upon my bed, and meditate on thee in the night watches.

Often in the nighttime when we are wakeful, our minds go back to the past and memories flood our thinking. Our memory seems to work overtime at night.

David had remembered the wonderful things God had done for him, and pondered on God's wonderful kindness to him. "Because Your loving-kindness is better than life, my lips shall praise You" (Ps. 63:3, *Amplified*). How dear life is to us. We make every effort to prolong it and care for it. But David believed that the lovingkindness of God was better than life.

In the barren places of our lives, in times of helplessness, we, too, can experience God's lovingkindness. As we recognize all that God has and is doing for us, what joy it will bring into our lives.

When we can't sleep, how often we begin to think of all the things we have to do, or we worry about our problems. The more we try to sleep, the wider awake we become. But David had learned a wonderful way of spending his sleepless hours at night. He had a wonderful occupation, remembering God and meditating on Him. His experiences with God were real. Thinking of Him in the night watches brought joy. He said, "When I remember THEE upon my bed, and meditate on THEE in the night watches" (Ps. 63:6).

This is wonderful occupation for our sleepless nights. We can think of all that He has done for us and meditate upon who He is. Instead of counting sheep, we can count our blessings, numbering them one by one. As we do this, our hearts will be filled with praise. What sweet times we can have with Him in the quietness of the night. What peace He will bring to us. It may be He has some special word to share with us for our encouragement and comfort. It may even be a gentle admonition.

Meditation is not dependent on books, methods, or on our own efforts. We are to meditate on HIM. "My meditation of HIM shall be sweet: I will be glad in the LORD" (Ps. 104:34).

Psalm 63: 7, 8

Because thou hast been my help, therefore in the shadow of thy wings will I rejoice. My soul followeth hard after thee: thy right hand upholdeth me.

David had much to thank God for. In the above verse he enumerates some of his blessings.

First, he had the SURETY of GOD'S PRESENCE. "Because THOU hast been MY help." Throughout his lifetime, David had experienced God's help. Not one of his needs had been too great for God's help. In Psalm 46:1 we are assured, "God is our refuge and strength, a very present help in trouble."

He often experienced the SAFETY of GOD'S PRO-TECTION. "Therefore in the shadow of THY wings." The overshadowing protection of God's wings of love and care constantly surrounded David. "He who dwells in the secret place of the Most High shall remain stable and fixed under the shadow of the Almighty (Whose power no foe can withstand)" (Ps. 91:1, *Amplified*). In our time of danger He is our Protector. "He shall cover THEE with his feathers, and under his wings shalt thou trust" (Ps. 91:4).

In his heart was a SONG of PRAISE. "Will I rejoice." One of the lessons we learn from David is his constant praise of the Lord. He didn't just praise Him on the bright sunny days, but on the dark and dreary days. God can give us "songs of praise," too, even in the night season. He can teach us to sing in our desert experiences.

He had SECURITY on GOD'S PATH. "My soul followeth hard after Thee." We are always secure as we cling to God through the difficult places of life. "My whole being follows hard after You and clings closely to You" (Ps. 63:8, *Amplified*). We are not to cling to things or people, but to God.

Then he knew the STRENGTH of GOD'S POWER. "Thy right hand holdeth me." The fear of falling is removed as we let God hold us by His powerful right hand. "For I, the Lord your God, hold your right hand; I, Who say to you, Fear not, I will help you" (Isa. 41:13, *Amplified*).

Surety, safety, songs, security, strength—these are all blessings from God for us today.

Psalm 65:2

O thou that hearest prayer, unto thee shall all flesh come.

The doorway into the secret place of the Most High is always open to the soul in need. Prayer puts us in contact with God.

Someone has said, "Prayer is a conversation between the soul and heaven." It has been likened to a two-way telephone conversation. I have noticed that when a person makes a call from a telephone booth he usually closes the door so that he can hear clearly. He deposits his money before he is connected to the line. Then he hears the dial tone and dials the number. The connection is completed and the business transacted.

In our prayer time with God we need to close the door to the things of this world so that we can hear Him speak. "But, thou, when thou prayest, enter into thy closet, and when thou hast shut thy door, pray to thy Father which is in secret." However, before we can dial the number, the price must be paid. God, through His Son, paid the price that we might have access to His presence. Jesus said, "No man cometh unto the Father, but by me" (John 14:6). We must accept Jesus as our personal Savior before we have the right to "dial" heaven.

We must "dial" correctly. There are certain prayer conditions to fulfill. "And whatsoever we ask, we receive of him, because we keep his commandments, and do those things that are pleasing in his sight" (1 John 3:22). Also read Mark 11:24; John 14:14; 1 John 5:14, 15.

There is an open line to heaven for us. When we have

accepted God's price and fulfilled His conditions for prayer, then we can dial with confidence, knowing that God is on the line ready to hear and answer us.

Psalm 65:4

Blessed is the man whom thou choosest, and causest to approach unto thee, that he may dwell in thy courts: we shall be satisfied with the goodness of thy house, even of thy holy temple.

Are there times when you feel no one appreciates you? No one really needs you? At such times, just remember, Someone does love you with a special love. There is Someone to whom you are very special—God Himself.

God has chosen us for Himself. "Blessed is the man whom thou choosest." We are accepted in the Beloved; we are very precious to Him. "While we were yet sinners, Christ died for us" (Rom. 5:8). God paid a great price for us. "But you are not like that, for you have been chosen by God Himself—you are priests of the King, you are holy and pure, you are God's VERY OWN—all this so that you may show to others how God called you out of the darkness into his wonderful light" (1 Peter 2:9, LB).

There are many important people today with whom we could never have an appointment. There are other people with whom we could have an appointment but it must be arranged far in advance. Yet the God of the universe has given us access into His presence. Through Jesus Christ we can come before Him at any time. We don't have to wait for a special appointment. We don't have to reach a certain spiritual level. The way is always open. ". . . and causest to approach unto thee. . . ."

What a privilege that He will make our lives His home. "As God hath said, I will dwell in them" (2 Cor. 6:16). Do we treat Him as a guest or is He at home in our lives?

Many seek satisfaction in material possessions. But these are only transitory. We can know what it is to be abundantly satisfied with His goodness. The Lord Jesus Christ is the only source of complete satisfaction. "He satisfieth the longing soul, and filleth the hungry soul with goodness" (Ps. 107:9).

He has chosen YOU that He might bring complete fulfillment to your life. Do you not realize how valuable you are to Him? Pause and praise Him for this.

Psalm 68:19

Blessed be the Lord, who daily loadeth us with benefits, even the God of our salvation.

A special day is set aside each fall to thank God for His blessings. However, as children of God, we should thank Him daily for His bountiful provisions. The psalmist wrote, ". . . who daily loadeth us with benefits. . . ."

One day as Jesus entered a village, ten lepers approached Him. Leprosy was a loathesome disease for which there was no cure at that time. Seeing Jesus, hope must have sprung up in their hearts. Perhaps they had heard reports of the miracles He had performed. They cried out, ". . . Jesus, Master, have mercy on us" (Luke 17:13). His heart was filled with compassion for them.

Jesus tested their faith. He said, ". . . Go show yourselves unto the priests . . ." (v. 14). According to law, a person cleansed of leprosy had to go to the priest to be officially declared cleansed. As the ten lepers obeyed Jesus, they were cleansed.

What joy must have been theirs as they realized what had happened to them. Now they were free to go wherever they wished.

Suddenly one of them stopped. He remembered the One who had performed this miracle. Quickly he returned to Jesus and with a heart filled with gratitude he fell at Jesus' feet in worship. "And fell down on his face at his feet, giving HIM thanks" (v. 16).

Jesus said to him, "Were there not ten cleansed? But where are the other nine?" Nine had gone their way—happy—but forgetful and unthankful. Their interest was in what He had done for them, forgetting the One who had performed the miracle. Only one returned to Jesus to express his thanks and worship Him.

We say, "How ungrateful!" But how many times do we, too, fail to thank God for what He has done for us? Do we take time to worship Him?

Why not pause now and thank Him for all the blessings He has given you, for material possessions and spiritual blessings. Thank Him for the trials He has permitted that He might teach needful lessons to you. "It is a good thing to give thanks unto the Lord, and to sing praises unto thy name, O most High" (Ps. 92:1).

Psalm 72:6

He shall come down like rain upon the mown grass: as showers that water the earth.

In this verse we read of rain which comes down on the mown grass. However we are told that the expression "mown grass" does not refer to the grass which has been cut but to the stubble which remains. As the rain comes down upon this stubble, it heals and revives it. The stubble begins to grow again, becomes green, and is eventually harvested. I have heard, in fact, that the second cutting of hay is usually better than the first.

God sometimes prunes our lives. This pruning leaves our hearts bruised and bleeding. Then the tender and gentle rains of His love and comfort come down upon these wounds. The Holy Spirit pours upon them the Balm of Gilead with its healing power. Rain on mown grass is not more gentle than His loving touch on human souls. The wounds begin to heal, growth begins again, and there is an abundant second crop to His glory.

A Christian had two cut-glass dishes. They were alike in size and weight, but one was coarsely cut and the other was finely cut. When the latter was placed in the sunlight, it sparkled with all the colors of the rainbow. The finely-cut dish was the more beautiful. The same is true of us. Many of us are not willing to endure the painful cutting process in our lives, but it can make us choice and beautiful vessels to reflect the beauty of our lovely Lord. "Now no chastening for the present seemeth to be joyous, but grievous; nevertheless afterward it yieldeth the peaceable fruit of righteousness unto them which are exercised thereby" (Heb. 12:11).

Psalm 73:26

My flesh and my heart faileth: but God is the strength of my heart, and my portion for ever.

Today many people are living in circumstances for which there is no way out humanly speaking—BUT

GOD. Some are experiencing storms so severe they are almost sinking—BUT GOD. Others have hearts almost breaking with sorrow and pain—BUT GOD.

In this Psalm the writer was confused and troubled. As he looked about him, there were many things he couldn't understand. Why were some people better off materially than he? Why did others seem to have less trouble than he? Yet he had tried to live for God.

The more he pondered this, the more he was bewildered at the seeming injustice he saw about him. Why didn't God do something?

His feeling of frustration continued UNTIL—he went into the sanctuary of God (Ps. 73:17). In God's presence the answer came. He discovered he had been looking at the problem from his own viewpoint. BUT GOD completely changed his attitude. He discovered God knew what was going on but God wasn't through with the wicked yet.

His problem was that his eyes were focused in the wrong direction. He had been looking at people and circumstances instead of the Lord. He had left God out of his thinking.

When he went into the sanctuary he saw things from God's viewpoint. He had been looking at the immediate, but God could see the ultimate. He realized God was still in control.

He said, "Whom have I in heaven but thee? And there is none upon earth that I desire beside thee. MY flesh and MY heart FAILETH: BUT GOD is the strength of my heart, and my portion for ever" (vv. 25, 26). He realized that God was all he needed. "Whom have I but thee?"

Burdens may press; disappointments may come. We may feel deserted. Family may fail us, friends may forsake. We may cry out, "My heart faileth." All may seem wrong BUT GOD is the One we need. "He is the strength of MY heart and MY portion forever." He is never unfaithful. He can turn our sorrows to joy, our distresses to deliverances, our trials to triumphs, our problems to praise.

Psalm 73:28

But it is good for me to draw near to God: I have put my trust in the Lord God, that I may declare all thy works.

Asaph was perplexed over the injustices of life. He became a "ruffled" personality as he considered the prosperity of the evildoers. Was it worth trying to live an upright life as he did?

However, his answer came as he went into God's presence. He realized he had left God out of his thinking. God wasn't through with the people yet.

Some wonderful assurances came to him. First, he was assured of God's presence. "I am continually with thee" (Ps. 73:23). No matter where we are or what is happening, we are assured of His presence.

God's power was assured Asaph. "Thou hast holden me by my right hand" (v. 23). I remember well the last roller coaster ride I had. It was considered a "thriller." On previous ones we had always been strapped in. This one only had a bar in front of us. The operator instructed us to hold on to the bar and not let go. When we began going up and down and from side to side, I was sure I could never hold on. About that time I promised the Lord if He would get me back safely I would never ride again, and I never have.

In our Christian experience I am glad we don't have to

hold on to God. We would not have sufficient power. He holds us and never lets go.

Asaph was assured of God's guidance. "Thou shalt guide me with thy counsel" (v. 24). When we do not know which way to go, or what decision to make, He does it for us.

Asaph came to a wonderful conclusion. "HE is the strength of my heart" (Ps. 73:26, LB). Our weakness becomes His strength. He is our portion forever, sufficient for each need each day of our lives. Asaph, a ruffled personality, became a restful personality, as he put his trust completely in God.

No wonder he could say, "But as for me, I get as close to Him as I can! I have chosen Him and I will tell everyone about the wonderful ways He rescues me" (v. 28, LB).

Psalm 78:53

And he led them on safely, so that they feared not.

I once heard about a group of children who had gone for a walk in the woods. Soon they realized that they were lost. The younger ones began to cry, but the older girl said calmly, "We are going to kneel and pray and ask God to lead us out of the woods." This they did. As they finished praying a bird lighted in front of them. The children attempted to pick up the little creature. Each time they reached for it, however, it hopped ahead of them. Soon the children were surprised to find themselves out of the woods and near their home.

So our Guide will lead us safely in the way we are to

go. Perhaps we cannot see ahead. We may be uncertain of the way. But the Holy Spirit will lead us step by step. He will not only lead us, but lead us *safely*.

With such a One to lead us safely, we need not fear. As He has safely led His children down through the ages, so will He lead you this very day. Life may continue to be filled with dangers and perils, but with our Heavenly Guide we need not fear. It has been said, "Safety is not the absence of danger but the presence of the Lord." Rejoice in the assurance that God leads His dear children safely.

Psalm 84 : 3

Yea, the sparrow hath found an house, and the swallow a nest for herself, where she may lay her young, even thine altars, O Lord of hosts, my King, and my God.

Both sparrows and swallows are mentioned in this verse. Usually sparrows are considered of little value. Jesus said, "Are not two sparrows sold for a farthing?" (Matt. 10:29a). But in Luke 12:6a we read, "Are not five sparrows sold for two farthings?" When four sparrows were purchased, an extra one was added without charge.

Without God, we, too, are of no value. "For I know that in me (that is, in my flesh) dwelleth no good thing" (Rom. 7:18a). Yet we are valuable to God—so valuable that He provided redemption for us. We may be as poor, worthless sparrows, yet we are the objects of God's love and grace.

We are told that the swallow is one of the most restless birds. It keeps moving most of the time, is never still. So, too, without Christ we are restless. We have no real rest apart from Him.

Altars (plural) are mentioned in this verse. In the Old Testament worship there were two altars. First was the brazen altar, a picture of the work of Christ on the cross. As the little sparrow found "rest" at the altar of God, so we find the "rest of salvation" at God's altar. Our salvation is complete, not in what we do, but in receiving what has been done for us. "While we were yet sinners, Christ died for us" (Rom. 5:8b).

There was also the golden altar from which arose the sweet fragrance of incense to God. This altar speaks of Christ and His constant ministry of intercession for us. He who died for me now lives to intercede for me and to present my every need before God. As the swallow found rest at the altar, so we can take our burdens and cares to our great Intercessor and leave them with Him. From Him comes the rest we need for living day by day.

"Be still and rest in the Lord; wait for Him, and patiently stay yourself upon Him" (Ps. 37:7, *Amplified*).

Psalm 84:5

Blessed is the man whose strength is in thee; in whose heart are the ways of them.

In these days when we are pressured on every side, we often wonder how we will make it through the day. We need a strength beyond our own limited supply.

It is encouraging to know there is strength available for us, sufficient for today's need. The source of this strength is God Himself. "Blessed is the man whose strength is in

THEE." The supply is inexhaustible, enough for everyone, and ready for us to draw upon at all times. We are not provided tomorrow's strength today, but we are given strength for today. The *Living Bible* (Ps. 84:5) reads, "Happy are those who are strong in the Lord, who want above all else to follow your steps."

Blessed also is the one "in whose heart are the ways of them." The words "of them" are in italics in the Bible. If we omit these two words we read "in whose heart are the ways." In the heart of the child of God are God's ways, His likenesses, His way of doing things. It is a heart guided and directed by God. It has been said, "God's ways must rule our hearts if our feet are to tread God's paths."

As trials come, we may find ourselves in the Valley of Baca, which means weeping. Our reaction to such experiences is important. We can become bitter, filled with self-pity, or we can let the valley be transformed into a blessing. "When they walk through the Valley of Weeping it will become a place of springs where pools of blessing and refreshment collect after rains!" (Ps. 84:6, LB).

Our tears can become wells of grace and springs of blessing. We might ask ourselves, "What am I leaving behind in the Valley of Weeping? Murmuring or complaining? Or praise and joy?"

In our physical life, we go from strength to weakness. But in the Lord, we go from strength to strength. Our strength may fail, but His is limitless. Paul wrote, "That is why we never give up. Though our bodies are dying, our inner strength in the Lord is growing every day" (2 Cor. 4:16, LB).

Psalm 90:1, 2

Lord, thou hast been our dwelling place in all generations. Before the mountains were brought forth, or ever thou hadst formed the earth and the world, even from everlasting to everlasting, thou art God.

What grandeur and majesty is expressed in this Psalm. Moses acknowledged God as the Self-Existent One, "even from everlasting to everlasting *thou art God*."

This was written of the wanderings of the Children of Israel through the wilderness. As they roamed about in the desert country, they must have longed for a permanent home. Often they must have wished they could settle down and have a feeling of security.

Moses, experiencing the day-by-day change of their desert life, looked beyond the changeableness of life on earth and wrote of the dwelling place that is lasting and permanent, that is unchanging. This dwelling place is God Himself.

God is a living God. He always was—and He always will be. He will never change. "For I am the Lord, I change not" (Mal. 3:6). And He is the same today as He was yesterday. He will not change tomorrow. Kingdoms have come and gone—people have come and gone, but God remains steadfast, unmoveable and unchanging. Through all the generations He has remained the same. Through all the generations He has been the dwelling place of His own.

Today our own dwelling place can be in this same God of the generations. God has made this possible through acceptance of Jesus Christ as Savior. Knowing Him in this personal relationship we experience the security of dwelling in the very God of the ages. What need have we to fear when He is our dwelling place?

"Lord, You have been our dwelling place *and our refuge* in all generations [says Moses]" (*Amplified*).

Psalm 90:12

Teach us to number our days and recognize how few they are; help us to spend them as we should. (LB)

Our lives are like a jewel case in which God has placed our days as jewels. From our jewel case He draws out a day, one at a time, and presents it to us to use.

As we begin a new day we accept the finality of our yesterdays. They are past. Paul wrote, "Forgetting the past" (Phil. 3:13, LB). We face the uncertainty of our tomorrows. "For the length of your lives is as uncertain as the morning fog—now you see it; soon it is gone" (James 4:14, LB).

But we have the reality of our present moment, our today. How will we use it? We can spend it on ourselves, on some cherished plan or desire of our own. Or we can present it to our heavenly Father to use in a way that will bring joy to His heart and glory to His name.

With the privilege of using God's today, why waste time brooding or longing over the past? It is gone. Why be fearful of tomorrow? It may never come.

Today, now, this present moment, is a special gift

from God. As we listen to His still small voice He will reveal how we are to spend it.

The psalmist said, "TEACH us to number our days." Someone asked Will Rogers how he would spend his days if he knew he only had a few left to live. He replied, "One at a time."

David wrote, "Lord, help me to realize how brief my time on earth will be. Help me to know that I am here for but a moment more. My life is no longer than my hand! My whole lifetime is but a moment to you. Proud man! Frail as breath! A shadow! And all his busy rushing ends in nothing. He heaps up riches for someone else to spend. And so, Lord, my only hope is in you" (Ps. 39:4–7, LB).

It has been said, "Tomorrow is God's secret, but today is yours to live. This is God's today; live it for Him."

Psalm 90:17

Let the beauty of the Lord our God be upon us.

Women spend much time and money on making themselves attractive. More important than outer beauty, however, is the inner beauty of life. This inner beauty of life is found in the person of our lovely Lord, Jesus Christ, Himself. He is spoken of as the One Altogether Lovely. His presence in our lives gives us this inner radiance. God desires that we be conformed to the image of the Lord.

This beauty of Jesus Christ is something we can ask for. "*Let* the beauty of the Lord our God be upon *me*." The transformation takes place in the secret place of His presence. "Strength and beauty are in his sanctuary" (Ps.

96:6b). As we behold Him we are transformed into His beauty and loveliness.

In St. Peter's Church, Cologne, hanging side by side, there are two pictures of the crucifixion of Peter. Early in the nineteenth century, when Napoleon ransacked the city, he took the original of the picture away. The artist painted another one to take its place. In time the original was restored and the two were then hung side by side. There is so little difference in them that one can hardly tell which is the original.

The Holy Spirit will do this in our lives. Christ, the Original, is absent, but the Holy Spirit will work in our lives conforming us to His likeness. Are we so nearly like the Original that people cannot see much difference?

Psalm 91 : 1

He that dwelleth in the secret place of the most High shall abide under the shadow of the Almighty.

Insecurity is a characteristic of many people today. They are constantly searching for ways to give themselves greater security. They purchase insurance to cover every conceivable kind of hazard. They install various kinds of protective devices to give safety in their homes. Yet with all these precautions they are still fearful and worried.

The above verse is a favorite Scripture. Psalm 91 has been called the "Traveler's Psalm," for its blessings can be appropriated for our journey through life. It is a hymn of trust and assurance. The Berkeley translation calls it "Divine Security." It brings words of comfort, peace, and strength.

In the midst of our worry and fear-filled lives, God has

a secret place where we can live with Him in perfect security. "Dwelleth" means to reside habitually with Him; it means to live in His presence. There we have a place of safety. No harm can touch us, we are protected from danger, and we are safe IN HIM.

"He who dwells in the secret place of the Most High shall remain stable and fixed under the shadow of the Almighty (Whose power no foe can withstand)" (Ps. 91:1, *Amplified*).

When the storms of life break on us we have a secret place where we can run for safety. When we are misunderstood, when false rumors are circulated about us, when we are deeply hurt by someone dear to us, we can hide under the shadow of our almighty God, and feel His comfort and understanding pour into our hearts. He can minister to us as no one else can.

There we find ourselves having heart to heart communion with God. In Song of Solomon 2:3 we read "I sat down under His shadow with great delight." "Sat down" indicates abiding there with no desire to leave His presence.

There in His presence we find protection, security, peace, and delight.

It has been said that "under the shadow of God's wing the little shadows of life are blended into His peace and thus lose their terror."

Psalm 91:2

I will say of the Lord, He is my refuge and my fortress: my God; in him will I trust.

Yesterday we considered the security there is for those who abide in the secret place of the Most High God.

The one who dwells in the secret place, "will say OF

the Lord, He is MY refuge, a hiding place from danger, and MY fortress, a defense against my enemies."

A refuge is a safe retreat from a pursuing enemy. A fortress is a tower of defense, standing firm to meet the attacks of the enemy. We have no power or might of our own to resist the temptations and trials that come. They are too strong for us. But in our safe place of refuge there is safety.

The picture of a mother hen gathering her chicks under her wing illustrates this truth. During a storm how quickly the little chicks run to the mother hen and hide under her sheltering wings.

Under His wing is security, stability, and safety for us. "He shall cover thee with his feathers, and under his wings shalt thou trust; his truth shall be thy shield and buckler" (Ps. 91:4).

He has promised those dwelling in the secret place complete deliverance. "He shall deliver thee"; He will protect from every danger. "He will cover thee with His feathers"; He will free you from every fear. "Thou shalt not be afraid;" He will keep you from harm. "No evil will befall you"; "No plague will come nigh thee."

God has promised some "I wills" for those abiding in Him: "I will deliver," "I will set him on high," "I will answer him," "I will be with him," "I will honor him," and "I will satisfy him."

When trouble comes and we run to Him, we will find Him our safe refuge. When opposition comes and we trust Him, we will find Him our fortress.

Spurgeon said, "We commune with Him, for He is the Most High God. We rest under the shadow of the Almighty God. We rejoice in Him as Jehovah, or Lord. We trust Him as El, the Mighty God."

This God is "MY GOD; IN HIM WILL I TRUST."

Psalm 92:12

The righteous shall flourish like the palm tree: he shall grow like a cedar in Lebanon.

In my early married life we moved to California. As we traveled across California at night, I remember the thrill of rousing from my sleep and seeing palm trees silhouetted against the sky in the moonlight. I had seen many pictures of them but this was my first view of a live palm tree. I still remember vividly my feeling of awe as I gazed at their stately beauty.

Someone has said, "The palm tree is God's portrait in nature of a Christian."

Certain characteristics of the palm tree picture the life and experience of a Christian. The palm tree stands above other trees, and is, by its nature, upright and stately. As Christians we are to manifest the righteousness and uprightness of God. "He that walketh uprightly walketh surely" (Prov. 10:9). How tall are we spiritually?

The palm tree is a tree of special beauty; it is one of the most graceful of trees. As Christians, our lives should reflect the beauty of Jesus Christ wherever we go. "And let the beauty of the Lord our God be upon us" (Ps. 90:17).

The psalmist said, "The righteous shall flourish." To flourish means to thrive, to prosper, to grow luxuriantly. We usually think conditions must be ideal for a luxuriant growth. However, the palm tree proves that this is not so. It grows in places not conducive to growth, providing an oasis of rest for travelers along the way. Where not much else grows we find the palm tree flourishing.

Christians can grow and flourish in the most trying conditions. Our present situation may not be ideal, but we can flourish there, for our Christian growth is not dependent on our environment but on the Lord.

The psalmist said, "And he shall be like a tree planted by the rivers of water, that bringeth forth his fruit in his season; his leaf also shall not wither; and whatsoever he doeth shall prosper" (Ps. 1:3).

Does your life show that you are a "palm tree" Christian?

Psalm 92:12

The righteous shall flourish like the palm tree: he shall grow like a cedar in Lebanon.

Now that we've compared the Christian life to the palm tree and considered its outward beauty, let's look at the inner characteristics of the tree that are an example of a Christian.

Most trees get their life through the sap that flows up the tree just under the bark. Not so with the palm tree. Its sap flows up the center of the tree, producing new life from the heart of the tree.

The life of the Christian comes from the life of Christ implanted in the heart. "That Christ may dwell in your hearts by faith" (Eph. 3:17).

We discover the palm tree not only grows but flourishes in the most unlikely places. Why? Because it has a hidden source of nourishment. Although no water may be visible, the tree sends down a large tap root with other roots deep into the earth, appropriating nourishment for the soil and searching out hidden springs of water.

We have hidden springs of Living Water from which we can draw nourishment. "If anyone is thirsty, let him come to me and drink. For the Scriptures declare that rivers of living water shall flow from the innermost being of anyone who believes in me. (He was speaking of the Holy Spirit, who would be given to everyone believing in Him)" (John 7:37–39, LB).

The palm tree can withstand winds and hurricanes better than any other tree, not because of greater resistance, but because they bend and yield. When the winds and storms beat upon our lives, we, too, can withstand their fury, as we bend and yield, submissive to God, allowing Him to bring good into our lives from them.

Many lives have been saved by finding water near the palm trees. God wants your life and mine to be the means of bringing others to the Water of Life.

When our lives are nourished at His hidden springs, they can flourish like the palm tree, displaying His beauty and uprightness. We will be able to live victoriously above our circumstances.

Psalm 100:4

Enter into his gates with thanksgiving, and into his courts with praise: be thankful unto him, and bless his name.

The Thanksgiving season is a special time of giving praise and thanksgiving to God. Once a year, a day is set aside for expressing thankfulness, but for the children of God each day is a day of thanksgiving. The basis of our thanksgiving comes from a personal relationship with Jesus Christ. "Thanks be unto God for his unspeakable gift" (2 Cor. 9:15).

As we enter into His presence we are to "be thankful" and "bless his name." We are to come before Him with thank-filled and praise-filled hearts. God's mercies are new every morning but it is easy to forget to thank Him. A thankful heart is not dependent on the material things we possess but on the blessings that come from the Lord.

As we pause to thank Him for the blessings of the past year, we must not forget to thank Him for the lessons we have learned through our difficult times. We are not to be thankful for just the pleasant, easy things, but ALL things. "IN EVERY THING give thanks: for this is the will of God in Christ Jesus concerning you" (1 Thess. 5:18).

Our thanksgiving is to be continual, not just on Thanksgiving Day, but each day through the year. "Giving thanks ALWAYS for ALL things unto God and the Father in the name of our Lord Jesus Christ" (Eph. 5:20).

Thanksgiving expresses gratitude for what God does for us. Praise is our attitude toward God because of who and what He is.

Praise comes from a heart satisfied with the Lord. A satisfied customer is one of the greatest assets a business firm can have. "He satisfieth the longing soul" (Ps. 107:9). Does the Lord see us as "satisfied customers" with hearts overflowing with thankfulness?

It has been said, "We're so concerned about tomorrow that we fail to be thankful for today." As we praise and thank Him at all times and in everything, the minor notes of trouble in our lives become major chords of triumphant victory. May our lives be such a hymn of triumphant praise to HIM today.

Psalm 103: 1, 2

Bless the Lord, O my soul: and all that is within me, bless his holy name. Bless the Lord, O my soul, and forget not all his benefits.

This Psalm is one of the great Praise and Thanksgiving Psalms of the Bible. David had evidently been thinking about God and of the blessings he had received from Him, and his heart overflowed with praise. It has been said that giving praise to God is the highest of all spiritual exercises.

First, God is the object of David's praise. This is not merely lip-praise. Prayer gets things from God; praise gives to Him. From the very depths of his being David lifts his adoration and praise to God for who He is and what He has done. Praise should be personal—"*O my soul.*" It should be fervent—"*all that is within me*"— "my inner life, affections, emotions, intellect and will." This is the outpouring of a heart in grateful praise to the Giver of all. Such praise and thanksgiving lifts one closer to the heart of God.

God is the theme of our song and the goal of our worship. This praise from our hearts will bring joy to the heart of our Heavenly Father.

After the psalmist has praised God Himself, he praises Him for all His benefits. So often we forget to thank Him for all that we receive from His hand of love. Have you ever made a list of your blessings, not only material, but spiritual? We take many of them for granted and forget that they are really from Him.

Handel said, "When I think of God, the notes seem to come dripping from my finger tips." Is your heart occupied with praising God? Are you remembering to thank Him for all of your blessings?

Psalm 104:33

I will sing to the Lord as long as I live. I will praise God to my last breath. (LB)

"Whistling in the Dark" was once a popular song. There is a real truth in the title. We have discovered from experience that "whistling in the dark" can lift our spirits in our night watches. When discouraged and dejected, music can encourage and strengthen our hearts.

Music has an important place in the Christian life. In the Old Testament, singers were especially appointed to serve God in His sanctuary. In the New Testament, Paul wrote of a "singing company." "As you converse among yourselves in psalms and hymns and spiritual songs, heartily SINGING and making your music TO THE LORD" (Eph. 5:19, *Berkeley*).

When Jesus Christ becomes our personal Savior, He gives us a new song. "He has given me a new song to sing, of PRAISES to our God" (Ps. 40:3, LB).

Then the psalmist says, "I will sing as long as I live." On the bright days and the dark days, the sad and the happy days, the easy and the difficult days, we will sing to the Lord. In Job 35:10 we read, "Where is God my

Maker, who giveth songs in the night?" We can have a lifetime of singing to Him.

Then the psalmist says, "I will praise God to my last breath." Today our hearts may be heavy. Our song may be gone. Praising God is an effective way of bringing back our song. The song of the heart, even though weak, catches the listening ear of God. Our spirits are lifted and our hearts overflow with joy. There can be a lifetime of praise to Him.

He says, "My meditation of him shall be sweet" (Ps. 104:34). Real meditation is thinking of HIM.

Then He says, "I will be glad in the Lord." The rest of our days, our lifetime, we can be glad in the Lord.

"I will bless the Lord at all times: His praise shall continually be in my mouth" (Ps. 34:1).

Psalm 104:34

My meditation of him shall be sweet.

As we considered the subject of true meditation yesterday, we found its source is the Word of God.

Meditation on the written word leads us to meditation on the Living Word, Jesus Christ. God, in speaking of His Son, said, "This is my beloved Son, in whom I am well pleased" (Matt. 3:17). He is the object of our meditation. Only as we come into His presence, shutting out all other distractions and quietly consider HIM, will we know real meditation.

When we occupy our thoughts with Him we realize we cannot begin to fathom the depths of who He is. However, the Holy Spirit can reveal new and greater depths of knowledge of Jesus Christ Himself. "Christ is the exact likeness of the unseen God. He existed before God made anything at all" (Col. 1:15, LB). "In him dwelleth all the fulness of the Godhead bodily" (Col. 2:9).

As we meditate on Him, we contemplate who He is and why He came to earth. We reflect on what He did for us.

A dear Quaker lady used to spend a half hour each day sitting quietly. She called it her "still" lesson. God invites us to some "still" lessons. He says, "Be still, and know that I am God" (Ps. 46:10).

There are rich dividends from meditating on Him—such meditation will be sweet. Could anything compare with it? How real and personal His love for us! Solomon said, "HE is altogether lovely."

As we meditate on Him, we are released from pressure and tension, and our hearts are filled with peace and trust.

Meditation on Him shall be sweet, for He is our priceless possession. Paul said, "Yes, furthermore I count everything as loss compared to the possession of the priceless privilege—the overwhelming preciousness, the surpassing worth and supreme advantage—of knowing Christ Jesus my Lord" (Phil. 3:8, *Amplified*).

Such meditation on Him leads us to worship of Him. We bow and say as Thomas did, "My Lord and my God" (John 20:28).

Meditation of Jesus Christ is for each of us personally, "MY meditation of him shall be sweet."

Do you take time to meditate? Is Jesus Christ the object of your meditation?

Psalm 105:4

Seek the Lord, and his strength: seek his face evermore.

Today many are seeking for satisfaction and happiness. Some seek it in pleasure; others in fame; some in financial security; others in social position. But searching in these places is futile, for none of them bring the inner peace that people long for. Only in Christ do we find real peace, a peace the world cannot give, nor can it take away.

So often we seek for the things He gives us, but God's Word says we are to seek HIM, not His "presents" but His "PRESENCE." "Seek the Lord, and his strength; seek his face evermore."

Today burdens weigh heavily upon us. Often we are so pressed in on every side that it seems all strength is gone. What a relief to know that when OUR strength is exhausted, we have HIS strength available. He is an unfailing source of supply.

Paul experienced the sufficiency of the strength which comes from God. God said to Paul, "For My strength and power are made perfect—fulfilled and completed and show themselves most effective—in [your] weakness" (2 Cor. 12:9, *Amplified*). Paul recognized the reality of it in his experience. "For when I am weak (in human strength), then am I [truly] strong—able, powerful in divine strength" (2 Cor. 12:10, *Amplified*). Sometimes God allows the pressures to come that we may discover how powerless and inadequate we are in ourselves, and that our dependence must be in HIM.

Not only are we to seek His strength, but His face. Many times our way is so dark we can't see ahead. At such times what comfort it is to seek HIM! "For God, who said, 'Let there be light in the darkness,' has made us understand that it is the brightness of his glory that is seen in the face of Jesus Christ" (2 Cor. 4:6, LB).

In order to see a person's face, we need to be close to that person. As we draw near to Him, the brightness of the glory of His face is reflected in our lives, and from our lives.

Be satisfied with nothing less today than seeking Him, His strength, and His face.

Psalm 107:7

And he led them forth by the right way, that they might go to a city of habitation.

The first time my husband and I went to New York City, the hustle and bustle of the huge metropolis frightened me. How would we find our way about the city and see the many things that were of special interest to us? A simple solution was arranged. We were introduced to a man who lived in the city. He became our guide, taking us on a personally conducted tour.

The children of Israel are pictured in Psalm 107 as travelers, lost in a barren desert, hungry, thirsty, and lonely. When they cried to God in their helplessness. He delivered them; He became their Guide as "HE led them forth by the RIGHT way."

Today we may be wandering travelers, lost in a wilderness of loneliness, disappointment, discouragement, despair, fear. We may be wondering whether we are in the right way. Turning to Him in our desperation, He is ready to become our PERSONAL GUIDE. We need not question His leading. His way is always the right way.

He knows where we are. What may be an unknown way to us is known to Him. It may not be easy; it may not be smooth. But His way is the best way. With Him we are safe.

Sometimes we become lost because we go our own way instead of God's. We must come back to the place where we left Him and be willing to again go His way.

How can we know the right way? We must have regular communion with the Lord, in His Word and in prayer. We must totally commit our lives to Him. We must hold nothing back. Then we must be obedient to the direction He reveals to us, even though we may not see more than the next step ahead.

With Him as our Guide, He will lead us in the way that will lead us to HIMSELF. In Him we will find complete satisfaction.

"For he satisfieth the longing soul, and filleth the hungry soul with goodness" (Ps. 107:9).

Psalm 107:9

For he satisfieth the longing soul, and filleth the hungry soul with goodness.

When Jesus appeared for the first time after the resurrection, on the first day of the week, He met Mary Magdalene. Mary had come to the tomb to see the body of the Lord, but the sepulchre was empty. Weeping, she peered into the tomb and saw two angels. "Woman, why weepest thou?" they asked. She answered, "Because they have taken away my Lord, and I know not where they have laid him."

She turned away from the angels and saw Jesus standing. He asked her, "Why weepest thou? whom seekest thou?" Mary supposed Him to be the gardener. Her eyes blinded by tears, she said, "Sir, if thou hast borne *him* hence, tell me where thou hast laid *him,* and I will take *him* away." Her thoughts were filled with *Him.* Christ was "all" to her; she was wrapped up in Him; she was completely satisfied with Him.

Are we as wrapped up in Jesus Christ Himself as Mary was? Are we completely satisfied with Him? Many times you wanted something—a new dress; a piece of furniture; a position; a home—and believed that if only you could possess it you would be completely satisfied and desire nothing more. Yet when you obtained it, you soon wanted something more. It did not completely satisfy.

When Christ becomes real and precious to us, we find that He is all we want. Someone has said, "Christ responds to special love, revealing Himself to the loving, waiting heart." *He completely satisfies.*

Psalm 107: 29, 30

He maketh the storm a calm, so that the waves thereof are still. Then are they glad because they are quiet; so he bringeth them unto their desired haven.

Occasionally I spend a few days at a motel close to the ocean. It is a beautiful spot, right on the beach, with a breathtaking view of the blue Pacific. Sometimes as I watch a storm raging out in the distance, I wonder about the ships that are being tossed about as the waves beat upon them.

The psalmist writes of the power of God that can control a great storm and can quiet the fears of those experiencing it. "For he commandeth, and raiseth the stormy wind, which lifteth up the waves thereof" (Ps. 107:25). In desperation they cried to the Lord and He brought them out of their distresses. He hushed the storm to a calm and stilled its waves. As He brought them to their destination, their hearts were full of joy. "Then the men were glad because of the calm; and He brings them to their desired haven" (Ps. 107:30, *Amplified*).

Today we may be in stormy waters tossed about by waves of trouble, heartache, doubt, or fear. We may have attempted our own methods of stilling the storm. We may have turned to people for help. Having found no human way of calming our storm, we may be almost ready to give up in despair.

However, there is a way of safety for us through the storm. Jesus Christ, our great Pilot, not only knows the way, but He can calm the storm and still the waves. W. Graham Scroggie said, "Storm-tossed seamen, needing tranquility, find a 'storm-stiller,' Jesus Christ."

Although our outward circumstances may be stormy, Jesus gives us that inner quietness of heart that steadies us in our storm-beaten lives. The psalmist said, "HE maketh the storm a calm, so that the waves thereof are still." Although the waves may beat against us, we have a God-given calm.

Is the storm raging in your life today? Are you almost sinking beneath its waves? HE will make YOUR storm a calm, bringing you to a desired haven.

Psalm 109:21

But do thou for me, O God the Lord, for thy name's sake: because thy mercy is good, deliver thou me.

Psalm 109 was written at a time when David was deeply disturbed. He was being falsely accused, apparently without cause as far as he could see.

David had learned not to tell God what to do for him. He prayed, "Do THOU for me." In effect He is saying, "Do whatever is best." Because he had confidence in God, he knew he could trust himself and his problems completely to God, for God would only do His best for him.

He knew that his extremity was God's opportunity. "But as for me, O Lord, deal with me as your child" (Ps. 109:21, LB). David was implying, "Lord, I am coming to You in my need. I don't know which way to turn, but I have implicit confidence in You; You choose what is best for me." David said, "But do THOU for me, O God, the Lord."

David confessed, "For I am poor and needy, and my heart is wounded within me" (v. 22). God, in His tender love, reaches down and applies His healing balm to broken hearts. "He healeth the broken in heart, and bindeth up their wounds" (Ps. 147:3).

Then he asked God to deliver him in such a way that everyone, even his enemies, would recognize God's power. "Help me, O Lord my God: O save me according to thy mercy: that they may know that this is thy hand; that thou, Lord, hast done it" (vv. 26, 27).

David concluded with, ". . . he shall stand at the right hand of the poor. . . ." How comforting it is to have a friend stand by in time of trouble. The Lord is even more to us than an earthly friend. He is especially near in time of need.

Sometimes we say to a friend in whom we have confidence, "Do what you think best." We wouldn't say this to someone we didn't know intimately and trust implicitly. This is the confidence we can have in God. Today, are we saying to Him, "Do what YOU think best for me"? A trusting heart CAN say, "Do THOU for me."

Psalm 118:8

It is better to trust in the Lord than to put confidence in man.

A pair of scientists and botanists were exploring in the Alps for some special kinds of flowers. One day they spied through their field glass a flower of rare beauty. But it was in a ravine with perpendicular cliffs on both sides. Someone must be lowered over the cliff to get it.

A native boy was watching. They said to him, "We will give you five pounds if you will let us lower you into the valley to get the flower." The boy looked into the valley and said, "Just a moment. I'll be back." He soon returned with a man. "I'll go over the cliff," he said, "and get the flower for you if this man holds the rope. He's my dad." Have we learned to trust the Lord as this little boy did his father?

Sometimes we find ourselves putting our confidence in man and what we think he can do for us. But man can let us down. Man can disappoint us. Not so the Lord. Needs may be pressing in but we can look up, trusting an all-wise, all-loving God to do all for our good and His glory.

We can trust the rope of our circumstances to Him. Man may become weary and let the rope drop; or he may be distracted or become impatient. But God never wearies of holding the rope. We can confidently leave it in His strong hand.

John Calvin said of this verse, "All make this acknowledgment and yet there is scarcely one in a hundred who is fully persuaded that God can alone afford him sufficient help."

Was he right? Do we really believe God can handle any situation? Are we willing to trust the ropes of our lives into His unfailing hands?

Psalm 118:24

This is the day which the Lord hath made; we will rejoice and be glad in it.

How often, at the close of the day, have you said, "What a day this has been! I should never have gotten up this morning"? Probably most of us have had this experience.

Our attitude at the beginning of the day can set the pace for that day. If we begin with a spirit of complaining, dreading our day's schedule, wondering how we will have the strength and wisdom to meet its demands, soon we become filled with self-pity and discouragement.

What a difference it makes if we first look into the face

of God as we waken. We can prepare ourselves for the day by committing it to Him; by asking Him to guard our conversation, actions, and thoughts, that they will be pleasing to Him; by taking time to tell Him we love Him. Remember that "THIS IS THE FIRST DAY OF THE REST OF OUR LIVES." We must ask God to fit it into His plan for us.

Each day offers new opportunities. There will be new choices to make, new decisions, new avenues of service for the Lord. It may even be a day filled with heartache and pain, a day filled with unsolved problems. How different our day will be if we begin with a rejoicing spirit, knowing it has been entrusted to us by the Lord!

God has given His promises to encourage us through the day. "And as the DAYS, so shall thy strength be" (Deut. 33:25). "The Lord is good, a strong hold in the DAY of trouble" (Nah. 1:7).

Yesterday, with its successes and failures, is past. We are not to look back. We can rest in the knowledge that tomorrow is still in God's hand. Only today is ours to live for Him. So it is important how we use it, for "Today is part of my life work." Our joy is not in the day, but in "the Lord" who made the day.

The psalmist said, "Every day will I bless thee; and I will praise thy name for ever and ever" (Ps. 145:2). "Every day" includes today. "A DAY TO USE OR LOSE."

Psalm 119:10

With my whole heart have I sought thee: O let me not wander from thy commandments.

A boy was applying for a job. The employer who was interviewing him said, "I suppose you have many outside interests and hobbies that are even more important to you than your work. You are probably interested in baseball, cars, and other things boys enjoy." "Yes, sir," replied the lad. "I like baseball. When I play it, I play it for all I'm worth. But when I am here, I'll be all here. I'm not big enough to be divided." He was given the position.

If we want to succeed in business we must put our whole heart into it. If we want to achieve top honors in any field it will cost us our time and effort. Our whole life must be dedicated to it.

Isn't it even more necessary to give ourselves wholly to God and His work? The psalmist says that he gave God his undivided attention: "With my *whole* heart have I sought thee" (Psalm 119:10); "I cried with my *whole* heart" (v. 145a); "I will keep thy precepts with my *whole* heart" (v. 69). Whether he was seeking God, crying out for help or keeping God's precepts, he did it with *all* his heart.

Do we seek *Him* in His Word? We need to consider whether we merely read it casually or whether we search it word by word, seeking *Him* in it with our whole heart.

Do we seek *Him* in prayer? Do we pause until our hearts are quieted in His presence? Is our attention given wholeheartedly to Him or are we thinking only of what we are going to ask of Him?

Do we seek *His* will or our own? Someone has said that sometimes by our manner of life we are saying, "*my* will be done."

As we seek *Him* with our *whole* heart in the Word and in prayer, we will truly *love* Him with our whole heart.

Psalm 119:18

Open thou mine eyes, that I may behold wondrous things out of thy law.

As I read God's Word I find in it many precious gems. Each morning it is such a joy to open His Book, read a few verses or a chapter, and ask Him to give me something new, fresh and precious for that very day. Sometimes it is a new thought from some very familiar portion. At other times it is a verse tucked away in a chapter that I have never particularly noticed. But, oh, how it sparkles and shines with new meaning as it opens up to me!

As a miner goes into the mine digging for ore, so we can go to God's Word each day to dig out some precious jewel or gem, some treasure or nugget with which we can enrich our lives that day.

"Uncover mine eyes and I will look—wonders out of thy law," is the literal rendering of this verse. The last phrase is said to be a kind of exclamation made by the psalmist after the covering had been removed from his eyes. God is ready to give us the treasures of His Word if we but ask Him.

"But as it is written, Eye hath not seen, nor ear heard, neither have entered into the heart of man, the things which God hath prepared for them that love him. But God hath revealed them unto us by his Spirit: for the Spirit searcheth all things, yea, the deep things of God" (1 Cor. 2:9, 10).

Psalm 119:28

Strengthen thou me according unto thy word.

The Bible is a dependable guide for life, for it always points in the same direction. We must not only read the Word but study it and search it. We must not study it haphazardly but purposefully.

We are to see Jesus in the Word. We cannot see Him in the flesh, but we can see Him in God's Word. "And these [very Scriptures] testify about Me!" (John 5:39, *Amplified*). Do you want to see the preciousness of Jesus more clearly? Then search the Word.

We are to grow through the Word. Food is essential to our physical growth; we must also eat if we are to grow spiritually. "Eat God's Word—read it, think about it—and grow strong in the Lord" (1 Peter 2:2, *Living Letters*). How many are anemic because they lack spiritual food? How many are suffering from spiritual malnutrition?

The Word equips us for God's work. "Every Scripture is God-breathed . . . so that the man of God may be complete and proficient, well-fitted and thoroughly equipped for every good work" (2 Tim. 3:16, 17, *Amplified*). The Word can produce works that are pleasing to God.

We are to study to be approved. "Study and be eager and do your utmost to present yourself to God approved (tested by trial), a workman who has no cause to be ashamed" (2 Tim. 2:15, *Amplified*). God's approval—not man's—is the goal we must seek.

Psalm 119:71

It is good for me that I have been afflicted; that I might learn thy statutes.

In this verse David states that affliction was good for him. As he reflects on God's dealing in his life, he realizes the reason for the affliction: "Before I was afflicted I went astray." He recognizes that God in His goodness has disciplined him, and he declares, "Thou art good, and doest good." Then he confesses, "It is good for me that I have been afflicted." David was grateful for God's discipline.

Some lessons are learned only in the valley of tears. God has to wash our eyes with tears so that we can see clearly. Without the trials we might have missed the sweetness of having God's hand of love wipe away our tears. I can remember that in my childhood days when I was hurt I would run to my mother and she would kiss away the tears. I felt her strength and love and was comforted. So it is with God.

Affliction has a place in God's training program. Norman B. Harrison said, "When God tests you He is honoring you with the opportunity of putting Him and His promises to the proof." The great George Mueller said, "The only way to learn strong faith is to endure great trial. I have learned faith by standing firm amid severe testing."

The story is told of a German baron who made an Aeolian harp by stretching wires between the towers of his castle. When the harp was completed, he listened for its music, but in the calm of the summer the wires were silent. When the autumn breezes blew, however, he heard faint sounds of music, and when winter came with its strong winds, the harp gave forth beautiful harmonies.

Psalm 119 : 89

For ever, O Lord, thy word is settled in heaven.

We live in a changing world. Because of the insecurity all around us we need a strong support. How reassuring it is to know that God's Word is settled, steadfast and unfailing; that it is always fresh, always new, always up-to-date.

David had been in distress and in his discouragement he turned to the Word. In his time of trial he experienced the comfort of the Word that was "settled in heaven."

Our God is unchanging. "Accordingly God also, in His desire to show more convincingly and beyond doubt, to those who were to inherit the promise, the unchangeableness of His purpose and plan, intervened (mediated) with an oath" (Heb. 6:17, *Amplified*).

Since God is unchanging, His Word, too, is unchanging. "This was so that by two unchangeable things [His promise and His oath], in which it is impossible for God ever to prove false or deceive us, we who have fled [to

Him] for refuge might have mighty indwelling strength and strong encouragement to grasp and hold fast thhope appointed for us and set before [us]" (Heb. 6:18, *Amplified*). Our Lord has promised, "Heaven and earth shall pass away, but my words shall not pass away" (Matt. 24:35).

Not one word of the Book has had to be altered; not a prophecy has ever failed. It is the Miracle Book. It is the one and only Word in which we can rest our destiny for time and eternity.

This same unchanging Word is available for us today. God's Word will uphold us day by day in every situation and need. We can claim His promises one by one, day by day, for situation after situation.

It has been said, "We can ease our aching heads on the pillow of God's promises and then rise up stronger."

Psalm 119 : 97

O how love I thy law! it is my meditation all the day.

What a privilege we have of being able to read the Word of God. Most of us have a number of copies of the Bible in our homes. We are reminded in the above verse that we are not only to read it but meditate on it.

One definition for the word "meditation" is "to think in view of doing." According to this definition, how much real meditation do we do? Do we hurriedly read the Bible as a habit, not thinking of what we are reading? Do we read it as a duty, because we think as a Christian we should? Or do we pause as we read it, meditating upon it with the view of appropriating it into our lives?

As we read and meditate on it, we need to assimilate it, digesting it that we may be nourished and grow by it. "As newborn babes, desire the sincere milk of the word, that ye may grow thereby" (1 Peter 2:2).

Not only are we to assimilate it for growth, but to practice it in our everyday lives. "But be ye DOERS of the Word, and not hearers only" (James 1:22).

David meditated on God's Word because he loved it, and he loved it because he meditated on it. He couldn't get enough of it. He meditated "all the day." It is important to be regular in spending time in His Word. We need to keep our minds saturated with it.

Paul challenged Timothy, "Meditate upon these things; give thyself wholly to them; that thy profiting may appear to all" (1 Tim. 4:15).

Meditation is not something we can do hurriedly. The Lord Jesus Christ is revealed to us from the pages of the Bible. Our meditation is to lead us from the Word of God to HIM. We are to consider HIM. Such meditation on Him brings us to our knees in humility and praise. Our hearts overflow with love.

With the psalmist we can say, "My meditation of HIM shall be sweet: I will be glad in the Lord" (Ps. 104:34).

Psalm 119:103

How sweet are thy words unto my taste! yea, sweeter than honey to my mouth.

Someone has said, "The Bible is God's Word to us. We are to read it to be wise, believe it to be safe, and study it to be approved. It is the traveler's map, the pilgrim's staff, the pilot's compass, the soldier's sword, and the Christian's charter. Christ is the grand subject, our good its design, and the glory of God its end. It should fill the memory, rule the heart, and guide the feet. Read it slowly, frequently, prayerfully. It involves the highest responsibility, will reward the greatest labor, and condemn all who trifle with its sacred contents."

How important is God's Word for our lives? Jesus said, "You search and investigate and pore over the Scriptures diligently, because you suppose and trust that you have eternal life through them. And these [very Scriptures] TESTIFY ABOUT ME!" (John 5:39, *Amplified*).

It is possible to read it and yet miss the personal application of it in our lives as they were doing. Jesus said, "They are they which testify of me" (John 5:39). They knew the Scriptures, but they had missed its most important purpose of revealing the Lord Jesus Christ as the Son of God, the Savior of the world.

Do you enjoy reading the Bible? Do you search for the many wonderful truths revealed in it about Jesus Christ? Are you becoming more like Him as you assimilate it into your life? Are you appropriating it into your daily living to meet your needs?

It is said that the silkworm grows to be similar to the colors of the leaves on which it feeds. Jeremiah 15:16 reads, "Thy words were found, and I did eat them; and thy word was unto me the joy and rejoicing of mine heart." George Mueller said, "The vigor of our spiritual life will be in exact proportion to the place held by the Word of God in our life and thoughts."

The psalmist said God's Word was sweet to his taste, even sweeter than honey. May our taste for God's Word never become dull.

Psalm 119:105

Thy Word is a lamp unto my feet, and a light unto my path.

My husband and I traveled a great deal. Before we took a trip, we always secured maps and studied them thoroughly to know the best route to take. In fact, we gathered all the information we could possibly obtain to make the trip easier and safer.

On one trip I had been informed that a certain highway was the best route. We came to a turn-off which I thought was the highway we were to take. However, I didn't check the map. Soon we discovered we were not on the right road. Instead of a wide paved road we were on a narrow, dusty road winding through the mountains. Not only did it take us longer, but it was a rough road. I should have checked the map. Official maps are wonderful guides, saving time and gasoline, if we use them and follow them.

We need spiritual illumination for our walk through life and God has provided it. The Bible is God's "official map" for our daily travel to show us the right way.

Foot lamps used to be worn at night. They were fastened on the toes and as the person walked, the lamp cast a light on the next step ahead. So God's Word is a lamp for our way, lighting our feet step by step for our immediate needs just ahead. We can be assured of its light on our path through life.

In planning a trip we plot our entire trip. Then we take it mile by mile. So with our trip through life. The light of God's Word gives the general knowledge of God's will for our way. Then the "foot" lamp of His Word lights up the next step ahead for our immediate needs.

Spurgeon said, "The Word of God is a lamp by night, a light by day and a delight at all times."

Psalm 119:128

Therefore I esteem all thy precepts concerning all things to be right.

When an old minister was asked to give his favorite text, he replied, "When I think of a favorite verse, half a dozen dear ones come to my mind. On stormy days I want a cloak; cold days I want the sunny side of the wall; hot days I want a shady path; now I want a shower of manna; now I want a drink of cool living water; now I want a sword. I might as well try to tell which is my favorite eye. The one I might love is the one I might soon need and want."

Perhaps when asked to give a verse, you always turn to the same one. When you open the Bible to read from it, you turn to certain favorite portions.

Yet one of my richest blessings in reading the Bible through is that over and over I find some rich little gem and nugget tucked away in portions where I might least expect it.

The above verse says, "I esteem *all* thy percepts concerning *all* things to be right," not just some of them; not just the ones I especially like; not just concerning the things that are easy for me to do, but all His precepts in all things. Second Timothy 3:16 says, "*All* scripture is given by inspiration of God, and is profitable for doctrine, for reproof, for correction, for instruction in righteousness.''

Psalm 119:130

The entrance of thy words giveth light; it giveth understanding unto the simple.

Have you ever entered an unfamiliar room in the dark? As you groped for the light switch, you may have stumbled over something. The furniture may have cast shadows in the room. You groped along the wall where you thought the switch might be. Suddenly your hand touched it and you snapped it on. How different the room looked as the light flooded it!

God's Word does this for our lives. Often we read and reread some portion of Scripture and suddenly one day it sheds a new light on some problem which is troubling us. Or perhaps some new experience in our lives imparts a deeper meaning to a Scripture verse or passage. All may seem dark ahead. We may be unable to see the way. We may desperately need a solution to a problem. Suddenly light shines from the Word and new understanding floods our souls.

Not only does the Word give light and understanding, but it is continually unfolding in our lives. The Holy Spirit is our Teacher and continues to reveal the Word to us and apply it to our needs. A Chinese scholar was once asked to read Psalm 119 in the original and then translate the 130th verse into the English language without consulting the King James Version. After studying the passage for a few minutes, he said, ''The Bible says; God speaks; a light comes! This makes a dumb man a wise one."

Psalm 119:133

Order my steps in thy word: let not any iniquity have dominion over me.

How many steps do you take in a day? By evening most of us feel we have taken too many. Regardless of the number, we only take them one at a time. A Chinese proverb says, "A journey of a thousand miles begins with one step."

The steps of our spiritual walk are important. If our steps are to go in the right direction, they must be ordered in God's Word. "Establish my steps and direct them by (means of) Your Word" (Ps. 119:133, *Amplified*).

When being trained for a new work we must first read and study the textbooks. We must absorb and familiarize ourselves with the subject matter. Then we begin doing what we have been instructed and trained to do. So in our Christian life. The Bible is our Book of Instructions. To walk in God's path, we must know His instructions from His Word. "The entrance of thy words giveth light; it giveth understanding unto the simple" (Ps. 119:130).

As we appropriate His Word into our lives, the Holy Spirit will guide our steps. "He will keep the feet of his saints" (1 Sam. 2:9).

A young pastor was impressed with his own knowledge of God's Word. He was invited to visit an older pastor who was not a great scholar, but was a real man of

God. The young man thought it would be an opportunity to display his understanding of the Bible. However, as the older gentleman picked up his Bible, he put his hand tenderly and gently on the opened page. The young pastor recognized the deep love this man had for the Bible and its Author, God Himself. This was the turning point in the young man's life. He realized his intellectual knowledge of the Bible was not enough. He needed the deep intimate love not only for the Bible, but for its Author, that the older pastor had.

Do you have a deep love like this for the Bible? Do you have a real desire to know its Author in a deeper, more real way? Do you desire that your steps be directed by it? "The steps of a good man are ordered of the Lord" (Ps. 37:23).

Psalm 121:1-2

I will lift up my eyes to the hills [around Jerusalem, to sacred Mount Zion and Mount Moriah]. From whence shall my help come? My help comes from the Lord, Who made Heaven and earth. (AMPLIFIED)

For years I lived at the foot of the Rocky Mountains. They never ceased to thrill me to the depth of my soul as I viewed their grandeur and majesty, and felt their power and strength. But even though I sensed the awesomeness of their beauty, my thoughts would go beyond the hills to the One who made them. With an UPWARD LOOK to God, I would meditate on His greatness and power.

The psalmist must have experienced this same feeling as he looked up at the hills surrounding Jerusalem, for he said, "My help comes from the Lord who made heaven and earth."

Today many people are facing problems for which they are seeking help. Some have been left alone; others are in a mental depression; some have physical handicaps. There are single girls who want to be married. Many are turning for help to tranquilizers, sleeping pills, pep pills, alcohol, and dope. Increasing numbers are seeking the help of counselors, psychologists, and psychiatrists. Although God may use people to encourage us in our time of need, the one sure source of help is the Lord Himself. "MY HELP cometh from THE LORD."

Are you in the valley of despair, disappointment, discouragement, or disillusionment today? Are you looking for help? Human sources cannot be depended upon, but real help comes from the Lord. We need to "look up" beyond our needs to the Lord Jesus, the One who can meet them. If He is powerful enough to create the heavens and earth, cannot He help us with our problems? He may not remove us from our desperate situation, but will lead us through it, if we keep our eyes focused on Him. He comes to us bringing comfort, pouring His healing balm into our wounds. His arms of strength uphold us.

"God is our refuge and strength, a very PRESENT HELP in trouble" (Ps. 46:1).

Psalm 121:3, 4

He will not suffer thy foot to be moved: he that keepeth thee will not slumber. Behold, he that keepth Israel shall neither slumber nor sleep.

In these days of world tension, what comfort and assurance we have in these verses! The Hebrew word for "slumber" means "to be drowsy." The Hebrew word for "sleep" means "to be off guard."

We may lose nights of sleep if there is illness in the home. When my mother was seriously ill, I was with her constantly, night and day, for three weeks, during which I had not more than an hour's sleep a night. Human love serves without ceasing. However, if we continue indefinitely without rest, our bodies will eventually be exhausted.

Not so with God. He never becomes drowsy and is never off guard. The Keeper of Israel neither slumbers nor sleeps. He never shuts His eyes to our needs. He assures us that He is never unaware of our problems. There is never a moment night or day when He does not see us.

One night a little girl was getting ready for bed. It was a moonlit night. "Mommy," said the little girl, "is the moon God's light?" "Yes," replied the mother. "It is God's light shining in the sky." "Will God turn off His light and go to sleep, too?" "No," the mother answered, "God's light is always burning; God doesn't go to sleep." "I'm so glad," answered the child. "While God is awake, I am not afraid."

Psalm 121:5

The Lord is thy keeper: the Lord is thy shade upon thy right hand.

Recently I listened to a commercial on television advertising the effectiveness of a certain burglar alarm system to insure safety for the home. We use various methods for providing safety and protection of life. We rent safety deposit boxes for our valuables, we deposit our money in banks, we insure our lives and possessions to protect from loss.

The psalmist had learned that beyond all human devices for safety, our one sure security is the Lord Himself. "The LORD is thy keeper." He can keep us in all places at all times. He guards us carefully, never relaxing His watch over us.

If we have to sit up through the night with a loved one we find it difficult to stay awake, but our Keeper never slumbers nor sleeps. There is never a moment when His eye is not on us.

If He is to be our Keeper, we must commit ourselves to Him. It has been said, "Everything is safe which we commit to Him, and nothing is really safe that is not committed." Paul wrote, "I know whom I have believed, and am persuaded that he is able to keep that which I have COMMITTED unto Him against that day" (2 Tim. 1:12).

Committal has been illustrated in this way. When we write a letter, we have confidence that the postal department will deliver it. So we write it, put it in an envelope, address it, seal it, and stamp it. We take it to the mail box. But we have not really committed it to them for delivery until we let go of it completely, and let it drop into the mail box.

Have you committed your life completely to His keeping, holding nothing back? Have you let go of your loved ones, committing them completely to God? Only as we let go of our lives and of those near and dear to us can God take over and bring His will to pass.

His keeping power is personal—THY keeper. It is a constant keeping. "The Lord shall preserve thy going out and thy coming in from this time forth, and even for evermore" (Ps. 121:8).

Psalm 126:6

He that goeth forth and weepeth, bearing precious seed, shall doubtless come again with rejoicing, bringing his sheaves with him.

We are living in a confused world where only a small percentage of the population have a vital personal relationship with Jesus Christ. The world truly is a field to be sown with the Word of God.

We are to *possess* this field for God—"He that goeth forth." The seed—the Word of God—is to be sown. In order to reap, we must sow. If we are to sow, we must go forth. The farmer doesn't stay in his back yard to sow his seed; he goes out to the field and scatters the seed.

We are to go forth "bearing precious seed" to *plant*. If no seed is sown, there will be no harvest. The amount of the harvest depends upon the amount of the sowing. "He which soweth sparingly shall reap also sparingly; and he which soweth bountifully shall reap also bountifully" (2 Cor. 9:6).

As we go forth, sowing the seed, we are to *pray*—"and weepeth." It has been said, "Seed doesn't grow very well in dry ground." Tears come from a heart of compassion and love. Our Savior had seeing eyes and a weeping heart. "And when he was come near, he beheld the city, and wept over it" (Luke 19:41). We need more than the mechanics of sowing; the seed needs the moisture of tears and the warm rays of love.

If we faithfully plant and pray, one day we will have the joy of standing before Him to *present* our sheaves, laying them at His feet. On the eve of the coronation of Queen Elizabeth, news was flashed around the world that a British climbing party had conquered Mt. Everest. Many attempts had been made, all ending in failure. But the climbers were undaunted. At last victory came. As their coronation gift of love and honor to the Queen, they presented their conquest of Mt. Everest. Will we have sheaves to lay at His feet—our love gifts to Him?

Psalm 127:1

Except the Lord build the house, they labour in vain that build it: except the Lord keep the city, the watchman waketh but in vain.

We often hear it said, "The strength of a nation is in the home."

Homes are made up of individuals, and the strength of the home depends on the strength of the individuals living in the home. So it is important that our lives be built on principles given by God Himself.

The building of our lives can be compared with the building of a house. In the building industry certain builders have gained a reputation for trustworthiness. People have learned that their houses are well built and give satisfaction.

We have the best "Builder" for our lives, God Himself. "Except the Lord build the house." His blueprints are "custom planned" for each individual life. His materials are top quality. He never makes a mistake in His building.

The foundation of the life He builds is Jesus Christ.

"For other foundation can no man lay than that is laid, which is Jesus Christ" (1 Cor. 3:11).

As we commit and trust ourselves to Him, He builds our lives in the image of His Son. "We are his workmanship, created in Christ Jesus unto good works, which God hath before ordained that we should walk in them" (Eph. 2:10).

At the time the construction of the Brooklyn Bridge was to begin, the engineer in charge became very ill. Each day he sent his wife with the blueprints. She checked to see that the construction was done according to specifications. At night she gave her husband a complete report, getting his orders for the following day. At last the bridge was finished. The engineer was sufficiently better that he was permitted to be taken on a cot to see the bridge. As he looked at it, tears streamed down his cheeks. "Oh," he said, "it is just as I planned it."

Are we allowing God to build our lives just as He has planned them?

Psalm 138 : 1

I will praise thee with my whole heart: before the gods will I sing praise unto thee.

David's praise was not halfhearted. He praised God with his whole heart. Have you ever praised Him for the following blessings as David did in Psalm 138?

1. His lovingkindness. It has been said that lovingkindness is love in action. God's lovingkindness was expressed by the gift of His Son.

2. His truth. We should praise Him for both the written Word and the Living Word. "Thy Word is truth"

(John 17:17). Jesus said, "I am . . . the truth" (John 14:6).

3. Answered prayer. "In the day when I cried thou answeredst me." We bring Him our petitions, but we forget to praise Him for His answers.

4. His strength. "And strengthenedst me with strength in my soul." This is not merely physical strength but inner strength to meet life.

5. Our privilege of hearing the Word. David said, "All the kings of earth shall praise thee, O Lord, when they hear the words of thy mouth."

6. His song. "Yea, they shall sing in the ways of the Lord." Do we sing in His ways, even though they are hard, even though they may not be our ways?

7. His glory. "For great is the glory of the Lord."

8. His respect unto the lowly. "For though the Lord is high, yet He has respect to the lowly [bringing them into fellowship with Him]" (v. 6, *Amplified*).

9. His refreshing in times of trouble. "Though I walk in the midst of trouble, thou wilt revive me."

10. His protecting hand. "Thou shalt stretch forth thine hand against the wrath of mine enemies, and thy right hand shall save me."

It has been said, "Praise is our highest exercise." In prayer we approach God for reasons which may be selfish; in praise, we adore Him for what He is in Himself.

Psalm 138:7

Though I walk in the midst of trouble, thou wilt revive me.

When I became a Christian, I thought my troubles would be over. I assumed Christians were free from trouble. But I discovered that even they are not immune. Job said, "Yet man is born unto trouble, as the sparks fly upward" (Job 5:7). We have not been promised exemption from trouble, but we are assured help in the midst of it.

David had learned to turn to God in his times of difficulty. Although deliverance wasn't always immediate, God's presence was with him in the midst of his trouble. Though he was surrounded BY trouble, he was revived IN it.

We read in Daniel of the king's command that for thirty days everyone was to worship him or be thrown into a fiery furnace. Because three men defied his command, they were thrown into a furnace heated seven times hotter than usual. Suddenly four men were seen walking in the furnace. The king said, "The form of the fourth is like the Son of God" (Dan. 3:25). When they were brought out of the furnace, the fire had not touched them, their clothing was not scorched, their hair was not singed, they didn't even smell of smoke. Even as they walked in the midst of the fire, God walked with them, protecting them until He delivered them.

How often we find ourselves in the midst of trouble. God uses this in the process of accomplishing His purpose for our lives. David didn't say, "The Lord CAN perfect," but "The Lord WILL perfect that which concerneth me" (Ps. 138:8). In the very center of our trouble He revives us and gives us fresh courage and strength to continue.

Someone has said, "In time of trouble say: 'First, He brought me here; it is His will I am in this place; in that I will rest. Next, He will keep me here in His love and give me grace in this trial to act as His child. Then He will make the trial a blessing, teaching me the lessons He means for me to learn, and working in me the grace He intends for me. Last, in His good time, He can bring me out again. HOW and WHEN He already knows!' "

Psalm 139:1

O Lord, thou hast searched me, and known me.

How many times have you said, "There is no one who really knows and understands me"? How many people really do know you? Do they know the person you want them to know, or the REAL YOU?

David said, "O Lord, you have examined my heart and know everything about me" (Ps. 139:1, LB). When He searches us, we cannot hide our weaknesses, mistakes, and failures from Him. Our lives are completely open to Him. He knows that which we try to hide from even our best friends.

The all-knowing God knows where we are and what we are experiencing every moment. He knows our loneliness, discouragement, and disappointments. He knows when dear ones forsake us. He knows when our world seems to be falling apart about us and there is nothing we can do. Nothing takes Him by surprise.

He knows our ordinary, everyday movements, even our sitting and our standing. He knows our inward thoughts even before they mature in our minds. "You know when I sit or stand. When far away You know my every thought" (v. 2, LB).

He plans our paths ahead. "You chart the path ahead of me, and tell me where to stop and rest. Every moment You know where I am" (v. 3, LB). The King James translation reads, "Thou . . . art acquainted with all my ways."

Not only does He plan our walk, but He accompanies us on it. He surrounds us with His presence. "You both precede and follow me, and place Your hand of blessing on my head" (v. 5, LB).

Today God knows us better than any person knows us. He knows us better than we know ourselves. He knows our innermost longings and desires. He knows our motives and our purposes, which often those nearest us do not understand. He knows our weaknesses and failures, yet He loves us with a steadfast and unchanging love. Not only does He know us as we are, but He knows the potential of what we can be in Jesus Christ. Realizing this, we can say as the psalmist did, "This is too glorious, too wonderful to believe" (v. 6, LB).

Psalm 139:3

You chart the path ahead of me, and tell me where to stop and rest. Every moment, you know where I am. (LB)

As we planned our vacation each year, we made careful preparations. After deciding where to go, a travel agency would chart our trip for us. It supplied us with maps of the area. Places of scenic and historical interest were marked. Included were suggestions for motels and restaurants, everything to provide for our needs on the trip. Having all this planned ahead made the trip easier and much more pleasant.

God has a planned path for each of us. In Jeremiah 29:11 (*Rotherham*) we read, "I know the plans which I am planning for you, plans of welfare and not of calamity to give you a future and a hope."

Not only does our heavenly Father know His plan for us, but He has it charted. "As thou goest step by step, the way shall be opened up before thee" (Prov. 4:12, *Free translation*).

Being an all-wise God, He knows the importance of "rest stops" along the way. Because He knows we may fail to take them ourselves, He includes them at the right places on our path for our benefit.

Not only does He give us rest stops to refresh us, but also to give us quiet times to think of Him and be aware of His personal love and care; to have a time of communion with Him. After Jesus' disciples had had a busy schedule, He charted a "rest stop" for them. "And he said unto them, Come ye yourselves apart into a desert place, and rest a while" (Mark 6:31).

Sometimes we feel God has forgotten all about us. But the psalmist had learned God never forgets. "Every moment you know where I am."

There is much instruction and encouragement in resting on God's Word. We can be assured there is rest for us today wherever we are, whatever our situation. This is not an outer rest of circumstances, but an inner rest of soul. "So then, there is still awaiting a full and complete Sabbath rest reserved for the [true] people of God" (Heb. 4:9, *Amplified*).

Psalm 139: 9, 10

If I take the wings of the morning, and dwell in the uttermost parts of the sea; even there shall thy hand lead me, and thy right hand shall hold me.

David not only recognized God was all-knowing, but that He was all-seeing. David said, "I can never be lost to your Spirit! I can never get away from my God! If I go up to heaven, you are there; if I go down to the place of the dead, you are there. If I ride the morning winds to the farthest oceans, EVEN THERE Your hand will guide me, Your strength will support me" (Ps. 139:7–10, LB).

Since God is everywhere, it is impossible to escape from His presence. It has been said, "There are no God-deserted spots." "He knows about everyone, everywhere. Everything about us is bare and wide open to the all-seeing eyes of our living God; nothing can be hidden from Him to whom we must explain all that we have done" (Heb. 4:13, LB).

Sometimes we try to fly away and hide from our problems, our circumstances, even from people. Yet if we fly with the speed of the morning light from east to west and reach to the farthest concerns of the world, we cannot get away from our pressures and frustrations. However, it is comforting to know that EVEN THERE in the midst of them He is with us. We may be in the depths of despair but EVEN THERE He will uphold us with His right hand of power.

Where are you today? Are you fretting about your circumstances? Are you trying to go your own way? Are you rebelling and resisting God's will? God is EVEN THERE waiting for you to let go of your own plans and let Him give you His. His are always best.

We must say as David did, "How precious it is, Lord, to realize that You are thinking about me constantly! I can't even count how many times a day Your thoughts turn toward me. And when I waken in the morning, You are still thinking of me" (Ps. 139:17, 18 LB).

Psalm 139:23, 24

Search me, O God, and know my heart; test my thoughts. Point out anything you find in me that makes you sad, and lead me along the path of everlasting life. (LB)

David realized that God knew all about him. "You . . . know everything about me" (Ps. 139:1, LB). Because he wanted his heart to be right before God, he asked for a divine examination. "Search me, O God, and know my heart; test my thoughts."

David asked God, "Search my life and show me anything that displeases You; even anything of which I might not be aware." David wanted an honest and open relationship between God and Himself. He wanted God to make a complete search—"me," "my heart," "my thoughts," "my ways." He wanted nothing to hinder his communication with God. David said, "He would not have listened if I had not confessed my sins" (Ps. 66:18, LB).

Are we willing for such divine examination and scrutiny of our lives? Do we say, "Search ME, O God, and know MY heart; test MY thoughts?" "Search me" means "God, YOU search me." True knowledge of self comes not from searching ourselves but from God's searching us, for He really knows our innermost being.

God may see a wrong attitude, a spirit of complaining or criticism that needs to be changed. A root of bitterness may have to be removed. We may be disobedient, self-willed, or self-seeking. We need to permit God to reveal anything in our lives that is hindering our spiritual growth. Not only is He the Great Revealer, but through Christ He gives us victory over our weaknesses.

David said: (1) "Search me." Am I willing for God to search me? (2) "Know me." Know my heart, my life, yes, even my thoughts. (3) "Try me." What are the results of this test on my life? (4) "See me." Does He see anything in my life that displeases Him? (5) "Lead me." In the path of everlasting life, the way that leads to heaven.

Life is centered around things that have either temporal or eternal value. May our prayer be that we not waste time on things that are transitory, but live each day with eternity's values in view.

Psalm 141:3

Set a watch, O Lord, before my mouth; keep the door of my lips.

If we could carry a recorder with us for one entire day, recording every word we say, and the recording were played back at the end of the day, I am sure we would be surprised and perhaps even a little ashamed at some of our words.

Psalm 141 was very likely written by David when he was fleeing from Saul. Evil things were being said about him. He was being slandered by his enemies.

He recognized his weakness and knew if he weren't careful, he could speak angrily to his enemies. He might say things he would be sorry for later.

So he asked God to guard his speech, to set a watch before his mouth, and to keep the door of his lips.

We, too, need a sentinel for our mouth to be placed as a

guard over each word before it leaves our lips. In unguarded moments we speak without thinking and say things we are sorry for later.

Failure to control our words is one of our greatest weaknesses, causing much harm. The moment we speak, others are affected. Words that go forth cannot be recalled.

The sentinel over our lips must guard carefully our hasty words, unkind words, untruthful words, impure words, harmful words, angry words.

Someone has given this good advice: "When we are hurt, keep still; when we are slandered, keep still; when we are impatient, keep still." If we wait a while before answering, our feelings may cool off and our attitude change.

Time brings a restraining effect, preventing a hasty answer.

Jesus gives us a good example. It was said of Him, ". . . neither was guile found in his mouth" (1 Peter 2:22).

We need to commit our lips to the Lord. They can become a blessing to God and to people. They can praise God and talk to Him in prayer. They can speak words of encouragement, kindness, and comfort to others to cheer them.

"Let your speech be alway with grace, seasoned with salt" (Col. 4:6).

Psalm 143 : 8

Cause me to hear thy lovingkindness in the morning; for in thee do I trust: cause me to know the way wherein I should walk; for I lift up my soul unto thee.

In the morning, when you waken, what is your response to the day? Do you want to turn over and go back to sleep? Are you grumpy? Does everything seem to be wrong? Or do you jump out of bed, ready for the day?

The psalmist gave a wonderful formula for beginning a new day. He said, "Cause ME to hear thy lovingkindness in the MORNING." We are to turn our thoughts to God first—THY lovingkindness. Do we begin the day thinking of God and His goodness to us? Or do we rush into His presence and out without becoming quiet enough to hear Him speak to us?

How different a day can be when we begin it with Him. The day may be dark and dreary, we may not feel well, we may be facing great problems and needs. But our spirits are lifted as we pause to praise and thank Him for His lovingkindness.

The psalmist reflects this as he says, "For I lift up my soul unto THEE." We read in Lamentations 3:22 and 23, "It is of the Lord's mercies that we are not consumed, because His compassions fail not. They are new EVERY MORNING: Great is thy faithfulness."

As we quietly wait before Him until we become confidently aware of His presence, we will be assured of His guidance for the day. "Cause me to know the WAY wherein I should WALK." We can hear His voice saying,

"This is the way, walk ye in it, when ye turn to the right hand, and when ye turn to the left" (Isa. 30:21).

What an encouragement to know that the day doesn't depend on us, but on Him—hear Him. Neither does the way depend on us—walk with Him. "Let me see Your kindness to me in the morning, for I am trusting You. Show me where to walk, for my prayer is sincere" (Ps. 143:8, LB).

Psalm 143:10

Teach me to do thy will; for thou art my God: thy spirit is good; lead me into the land of uprightness.

David was a man who lived in close companionship with God. God was very real to him. In the first part of Psalm 143 he brings his needs to God. He prays, "Hear my prayer, O Lord, give ear to my supplications" (v. 1). "Hear me speedily, O Lord: my spirit faileth" (v. 7).

David began his day with God, asking God to speak to him, "Cause me to hear thy lovingkindness in the morning" (v. 8). How eagerly he must have come into God's presence each morning to hear God's Word for him for that day. He had learned not to do all the talking. He said, "Cause me to HEAR." Do we take time each day to hear Him speak to us? Is our daily prayer, "Cause ME to hear"?

Then he asked God to guide his steps in the way he should go. "Cause me to know the way wherein I should walk; for I lift up my soul unto thee" (v. 8). There must be coordination between our ears and our feet. Not only should our ears be tuned to hear Him, but our feet should be obedient to follow His directions.

David's difficult experiences brought him to the place of complete dependence upon God. Not only did he pray to know God's will, but that he might walk in it. "Teach me to DO thy will; for thou art my God. . . ." He asked God not only to be his Teacher, but to be his Guide. "Lead me."

Because his confidence was in God, because he had assurance of knowing, "Thou art MY GOD," he could trust God to teach him and lead him in His ways.

Is our request of God for today, "TEACH ME—LEAD ME"? We should not only ask God to teach us to do His will, but also to lead us in conformity to it. It is more than KNOWING God's will; it is WALKING in obedience to His will.

Martin Luther said, "I may not know the way, but well do I know my Guide on the way."

Psalm 144 : 9

I will sing a new song unto thee, O God; upon a psaltery and an instrument of ten strings will I sing praises unto thee.

One night at a prayer meeting an old man prayed, "Lord, we will praise Thee with our instruments of ten strings." People in the service wondered what the ten strings were. He prayed on. "We will praise Thee with our eyes by looking only unto Thee. We will praise Thee with our ears by listening only to Thy voice. We will praise Thee with our hands by working in Thy service. We will praise Thee with our feet by running in the way of Thy commandments. We will praise Thee with our tongues by bearing testimony of Thy lovingkindness.

We will praise Thee with our hearts by loving only Thee."

We can praise God best by placing our ten-stringed instruments in His hands and allowing Him to play His melody of life. First we are to praise Him with our eyes—we are to look to Him, focusing our eyes upon Him. "Looking unto Jesus the author and finisher of our faith" (Heb. 12:2). Life has true meaning and purpose when our eyes are filled with the vision of Him. We praise Him with our ears by listening to His voice. Samuel said, "Speak; for thy servant heareth" (1 Sam. 3:10). We praise Him with our hands by using them for Him. "Whatsoever thy hand findeth to do, do it with thy might" (Eccl. 9:10a). We praise Him with our feet by walking on errands for Him. "How beautiful upon the mountains are the feet of him that bringeth good tidings, that publisheth peace" (Isa. 52:7a). We praise Him with our tongues by telling others of Him. "That which we have seen and heard declare we unto you" (1 John 1:3a). We praise Him with our hearts by loving Him. "Whom having not seen, ye love" (1 Peter 1:8a).

Instruments of ten strings—our lives—in tune with God and available to Him for His use will bring praise to His name.

Psalm 145 : 2

Every day [with its new reasons] will I bless You—affectionately and gratefully praise You; yes, I will praise Your name for ever and ever. (AMPLIFIED)

This is a Psalm full of thanksgiving and praise, extolling the One who alone is worthy of praise. David said, "I will bless YOU; I will praise YOU." His praise was not just for what God gave him or did for him, but for God Himself. He expressed his personal relationship to the One whom he praises, "MY God, the king."

His praise to God is continual—"EVERY DAY will I bless YOU—affectionately and gratefully praise you." There is an interesting phrase in this verse—"Every day WITH ITS NEW REASONS." That includes today. Sometimes we feel that we have nothing to praise Him for. But if we look for them there will always be new reasons for praising Him.

The psalmist's heart was full of GREAT PRAISE to a GREAT GOD. "Great is the Lord and highly to be praised, and His greatness is [so vast and deep so to be] unsearchable" (Ps. 145:3, *Amplified*). He is so great that we cannot explain or fathom it. "How great he is! His power is absolute! His understanding is unlimited" (Ps. 147:5, LB).

Our praise is to be never ending. "I will bless Your name for ever and ever" (Ps. 145:1, *Amplified*).

Regardless of our circumstances, conditions, environment, or needs, we have new reasons each day for praising Him. We are assured of His unchanging love for us. "I have loved thee with an everlasting love" (Jer. 31:3). We are assured of His constant presence with us. "I will never leave thee, nor forsake thee" (Heb. 13:5). We are assured of His willingness to work out each circumstance in our lives for our good and His glory. "And we know that all things work together for good to them that love God, to them who are the called according to His purpose" (Rom. 8:28).

The psalmist ends Psalm 145 with a great finale of praise. "My mouth shall speak the praise of the Lord, and let all flesh bless—affectionately and gratefully praise—

His holy name for ever and ever" (v. 21, *Amplified*).
PRAISE YE THE LORD!

Psalm 145 : 14

The Lord upholdeth all that fall, and raiseth up all those that be bowed down.

David had known God for a long time. He had seen His handiwork in the world about him. David had often communed with God. Many times he had experienced His loving and protecting care.

In this Psalm, David's heart overflows in praise to God. "I will praise You, my God and King, and bless Your name each day and forever" (v. 1, LB). He cannot comprehend the greatness of God. He says, "Great is Jehovah! Greatly praise Him! His greatness is beyond discovery!" (v. 3).

He rejoices in the personal concern of this same God for His own children. "The Lord upholds all those [of His own] who are falling, and raises up all those who are bowed down" (v. 14, *Amplified*). "The Lord lifts the fallen and those bent beneath their loads" (v. 14, LB).

What an encouragement it is to us to know that the God whom David praises for His greatness and goodness is ever mindful of us. Today He is personally concerned for you and me. He feels with us the grief we are experiencing. When our burdens almost overwhelm us, He is waiting to uphold us, and raise us up. He is always near to comfort and strengthen.

From His open hand He provides for our needs. "The eyes of all wait for You—looking, watching, and expecting; and You give them their food in due season. You open Your hand, and satisfy every living thing with favor" (vv. 15, 16, *Amplified*).

One day a little boy was in a grocery store. The owner told him to reach in the case and take a handful of candy. The little fellow hesitated. Then the man reached in, took a handful and gave it to the boy. Later, the boy said to his mother, "I knew his hand was bigger than mine."

David closed the Psalm with, "My mouth shall speak the praise of the Lord, and let all flesh bless—affectionately and gratefully praise—His holy name for ever and ever" (v. 21, *Amplified*).

Psalm 147:3

He healeth the broken in heart, and binds up their wounds.

For many years there was a company in Denver that had a fine reputation for mending china and glassware. They could restore it so perfectly you couldn't find where the break had been.

Life is filled with heartaches and sorrow today. Behind many a smile is a broken heart. Burdens come, one upon another, until we are almost crushed by their weight. Some beautiful dream you had looked forward to with such hope may have dissipated. You may be overcome with loneliness. Your heart may be broken and you cannot understand what has happened. We are not promised we will have an easy or comfortable life. Jesus said, "In the world ye shall have tribulation" (John 16:33).

But there is Someone who sees our broken hearts and lovingly understands. The Lord Jesus is the "Mender of

Broken Hearts." He sees them and is ready to pour His healing balm into them and bind up our wounds.

A cathedral in Europe had a beautiful stained glass window. During a storm it was shattered, breaking into many small pieces. The pieces were carefully gathered up and packed away.

One day a stranger came to the village. He had heard of the broken window and asked if he might have the pieces. He said he could restore the window to its former beauty, but he must have all the pieces. Since the villagers had no use for them, they let him take them.

Nothing was heard from him for months. Then one day he returned with the window. After placing it in the cathedral, he invited the people to come and view it. They gazed in amazement at its loveliness. No one could tell it had been broken. In fact, it was even more beautiful than it had been before.

Today your heart may be broken. The Lord Jesus can restore it, bringing new beauty out of it, but you must give Him ALL the pieces.

"The Lord is nigh unto them that are of a broken heart" (Ps. 34:18).

In Revelation 21:4 we read, "And God shall wipe away all tears from their eyes."

Psalm 147 : 5

Great is our Lord, and of great power: his understanding is infinite.

It has been said, "God is great in great things, but very great in little things."

A group of people stood on the Matterhorn admiring the sublimity of the scene when a gentleman produced a pocked microscope and having caught a fly, placed it under the glass. He reminded them that the legs of a fly in England were naked. Then he called attention to the legs of this little fly which were thickly covered with hair, thus showing that the same God who made the lofty Swiss mountains, attended to the comforts of the tiniest of His creatures, even providing socks and mittens for the little fly whose home was in these mountains.

In the first few verses of this Psalm we read of the God who is great enough to number the stars and call them by name. Although the scientist has studied the wonderful things of the universe with his telescope, he has never been able accurately to count all the stars. But God has.

Yet the God who can count and name the stars has a heart of love for the individual—for you and me. He who is great enough to do all this is also great enough to heal the broken-hearted and bind up their wounds, (v. 3) and to lift up the meek (v. 6). He has a loving concern for all His dear children.

Are you brokenhearted today? He will pour the Balm of Gilead into your heart bringing healing to it. Have you been wounded? He has promised to bind tenderly and lovingly each of your wounds. Are you bowed down by grief or trouble? The Lord Himself will lift up the meek.

Place yourselves with all of your needs in His all-wise care and keeping.

My Response

After reading these psalms of David, you may be wondering how you can know the Good Shepherd as your shepherd. If this is your desire, invite Jesus Christ into your life so you, too, can say, "The Lord is MY shepherd."

My Commitment to Jesus Christ

I *believe* Jesus Christ, the Son of God, gave His life on the cross to free me from the penalty of sin and give me forgiveness.

I *invite* Jesus Christ into my life as Savior and Lord.

I *accept* Jesus Christ as God's gift of eternal life.

My Prayer

Dear Lord Jesus:

I confess my need of a Savior. I believe You died on the cross to pay the penalty of my sin. I invite You into my life as my personal Savior and Lord. Thank You for Your gift of eternal life, which I have just now received.

In Jesus' name I pray, amen.

Signed _____

Date _____

Your signature and today's date will remind you of this moment when you received Christ as Savior. It will indicate your sincerity in this transaction between you and God.